DOLLARS & NONSENSE

Correcting the News Media's Top Economic Myths

Edited by

Stephen Moore ~ Club for Growth
Richard Noyes ~ Media Research Center

BRINGING POLITICAL BALANCE
AND RESPONSIBILITY TO THE MEDIA

PUBLISHED 2001 BY THE
MEDIA RESEARCH CENTER
BRINGING POLITICAL BALANCE AND
RESPONSIBILITY TO THE MEDIA

MEDIA RESEARCH CENTER
325 SOUTH PATRICK STREET
ALEXANDRIA, VIRGINIA 22314
(703) 683-9733
(800) 672-1423

www.MediaResearch.org

ISBN 0-9627348-4-5
Printed in the United States of America
First Edition

Second Printing, March, 2002
First Printing, October, 2001

TABLE OF CONTENTS

LIST OF FIGURES

LIST OF TABLES

ABOUT THE AUTHORS

Milton Friedman, winner of the Nobel Prize in economics in 1976, is a senior research fellow at the Hoover Institution at Stanford University. Dr. Friedman is the author of many books and articles, among them *Capitalism and Freedom*, which he coauthored with his wife, Rose D. Friedman.

Lawrence Kudlow is CEO of Kudlow & Co., LLC, and an economics commentator for CNBC.

Arthur Laffer is the president of A.B. Laffer and Associates and a former member of President Ronald Reagan's Economic Policy Advisory Board.

Stephen Moore is the president of the Club for Growth and a senior fellow at the Cato Institute. He is the co-author of *It's Getting Better All the Time: 100 Greatest Trends of the Past 100 Years.*

Brian Wesbury is first vice president and chief economist at Griffin, Kubik, Stephens & Thompson, Inc. He is the author of *The New Era of Wealth*, published in 1999 by McGraw Hill.

Nicholas Eberstadt holds the Henry Wendt Chair in Political Economy at the American Enterprise Institute and is a longtime member of the Harvard University Center for Population and Development Studies. He is the author of *Prosperous Paupers and Other Population Problems,* published in 2000 by AEI Press.

William A. Niskanen is chairman of the Cato Institute and a former economic advisor to President Ronald Reagan.

W. Michael Cox is vice president and chief economist at the Federal Reserve Bank of Dallas. He is the author of *Myths of Rich and Poor: Why We're Better Off Than We Think,* published in 1999 by Basic Books.

Robert W. Crandall is a senior fellow in the Economic Studies Program at the Brookings Institution. He is the author, with Leonard Waverman, of *Who Pays for Universal Service? When Telephone Subsidies Become Transparent;* and *Talk Is Cheap: The Promise of Regulatory Reform in North American Telecommunications.*

William G. Gale is the Joseph A. Pechman Fellow in the Economic Studies Program at the Brookings Institution.

David Hale is global chief economist of the Zurich Group.

PREFACE

◆

It is often said that the mainstream news media present audiences with a biased, distorted or overly-simplistic view of how politics, economics, and business truly work. Nailing down the facts of bias – *Did the reporter really say that?* – is a painstaking and tedious task, eschewed by many of those who raise their voices against one-sided journalism. Yet sifting through the fine print of newspapers, magazines and network transcripts, and fast-forwarding and rewinding miles of videotape, remains the essential work of media critics who wish their arguments to be taken seriously.

The Media Research Center (MRC), founded by L. Brent Bozell III in 1987, has done more than any other group to assiduously identify, expose and correct the pro-liberal, anti-conservative and anti-free market bias which contaminates much of the mainstream media's everyday news coverage. The MRC's archives currently hold more than 130,000 hours of news programming, all coded, catalogued and computerized by a team of dedicated and outstanding news analysts. MRC's signature publications – *Media Watch, Notable Quotables, CyberAlert,* and the *Media Reality Check* – provide more than a dozen years worth of extensive, irrefutable documentary evidence of the establishment media's liberal bias.

In 1992, the MRC launched the Free Enterprise and Media Institute, which later became the Free Market Project (FMP). For nearly a decade, the FMP has been the only organization in the world dedicated to the unique challenge of correcting misconceptions in the media about free enterprise; its regular newsletter, *MediaNomics*, along with a series of in-depth Special Reports, have provided the truth about the establishment media's bias against the free-enterprise system.

FMP Special Reports have documented some of the basic economic facts that are commonly excluded from the evening news: federal income taxes fall mainly on a small slice of wealthy Americans; domestic spending has increased every year, in spite of politicians' claims that they believe in "fiscal discipline;" and government mandates which raise the cost of health insurance for employers have increased the number of Americans who lack health care coverage. In an effort to help reporters craft more balanced news stories, FMP has worked over the years to promote the ideas and research of a wide variety of respected free-market experts.

This volume builds upon the past work of the Free Market Project by presenting, in a clear and concise manner, the truth about many of the media's most common misrepresentations of economic fact and theory. Ten of the most prominent free-market economists in the country – Milton Friedman, Lawrence Kudlow, Arthur Laffer, Brian Wesbury, Nicholas Eberstadt, William Niskanen, Michael Cox, Robert Crandall, William Gale and David Hale – have lent their time and their talent to this important project. Their considerable experience and expertise gives their conclusions an authority that cannot be easily dismissed.

We believe that economic and financial reporters all over America will find this book a useful resource, and we hope that the result is more informed, nuanced and balanced coverage of the major economic issues facing the nation today.

Stephen Moore
President, The Club for Growth

Richard Noyes
Director, MRC's Free Market Project

INTRODUCTION

◆

Economic Illiteracy in the Newsroom

The News Media's Most Common Economic Myths

Stephen Moore

*Practical men, who believe themselves to be quite exempt
from any intellectual influences, are usually the
slaves of some defunct economist.*
— John Maynard Keynes

Mark Twain once quipped to an adversary he was debating: "It's not what you don't know that's so dangerous. It's the things you think you know that just ain't so."

Twain could easily have been talking about the modern-day news media who are responsible for informing the public about economics and finances in America.

It is a strange paradox that while the U.S. economy has performed better than ever during the past two decades, the media's coverage of the economy is in some ways worse than ever. With the exception of a few outstanding financial reporters, there exists what can only be described as a state of widespread economic illiteracy in journalism today. And all of this at the same time when the quality of financial news should be excellent.

After all, the public's demand for first-rate economic and financial news and analysis has never been greater, thanks to the burgeoning new investor class of Americans. Twenty years ago, only about one in six American households owned stock. Today more than half do. The real financial wealth of the typical American household has more than doubled in the past 15 years. Business ownership rates, especially among women, have tripled since 1980.

The news media do a respectable job of reporting the hard facts – the Federal Reserve's interest-rate changes, unemployment reports, and stock market updates. But economic journalism is deficient in explaining and analyzing the how and why of our modern market economy. Perhaps the most pervasive and infuriating fallacy is that good economic news is portrayed as bad news and bad economic news is seen as good news. The public is force-fed this crazy, upside-down storyline virtually every day. We are inundated with nonsensical headlines like the following:

- *Economy Creates a Record Number of New Jobs; Report Sends Jitters Through Wall Street*
- *Wages Rise; Economists Warn of a Rekindling of Inflation*
- *Consumer Spending Soars; Fed Worries Economy Is Overheating*
- *Surge in the Dollar Has Economists Nervous About Trade Deficit*
- *Fall in the Dollar Welcome Sign that Torrid Economy Is Slowing Down*
- *Slowdown in Manufacturing May Allow Fed to Keep Interest Rates Low*
- *New Home Sales Fall to Lowest Level in Five Years; Relieved Analysts See Soft Landing for Economy*
- *Tax Cuts Could Do More Harm Than Good for U.S. Economy*

The public reacts to such "news" by scratching their heads in total bafflement, as well it should. None of the above headlines makes any sense whatsoever. For the past 15 years, the economy has performed brilliantly: new jobs have meant not more inflation, but less inflation; wage increases have not caused the economy to overheat; and a strong dollar has been a trophy of American economic strength, not a sign of weakness.

When the economy creates more jobs, there is no "but" or "however." A fall in unemployment is always and unequivocally good news – and should be reported as such. Virtually every report of encouraging economic news over the past decade has been associated with subsequent rises in stock prices over the weeks and months to follow, not declines. If only the media would simply present these developments right side up – good news really is good news and bad news really is bad news – the quality of economic reporting, and the public's understanding, would improve.

So what explains the economic mythology that passes for news these days? One factor is that when it comes to covering the U.S. economy, journalists are heavily influenced by a herd mentality. Wrongheaded ideas – such as the notion of an inevitable trade-off between inflation and unemployment, or the idea that the trade deficit is a meaningful economic measure – are so commonplace that it may seem impossible to wrench them out of standard news coverage and analysis.

But the economics profession itself is partly to blame for the substandard state of economic journalism. Many of today's economic reporters and editors came of age during the 1960s and 1970s when economics was in a state of confusion. During that era, academic economists traveled down the dead-end path of neo-Keynesianism. But while most academics have advanced beyond the prevailing theories and ideas of that time, a whole generation of college students wasn't rehabilitated after this disastrous misadventure in Keynesianism. Thus, journalists who had the misfortune to come of age during this era were never properly exposed to some very basic and universal lessons of economics.

If every journalist in America were simply required to read Henry Hazlitt's short but invaluable classic, *Economics in One Lesson*, the profession (and the public) might arguably be better served than from all of the collective economics courses they studied in high school and college.

But our objective is not to criticize or assign blame. Rather, we hope to provide some practical guidelines to help print and broadcast news reporters and editors improve their coverage of the modern American economy. For this volume, we asked a panel of distinguished economists to explain the facts behind some of the most common economic myths perpetuated by the media. While the economists we have selected to participate in this project unanimously favor free markets, we are confident that the preponderance of respected economists would agree with the their conclusions. And we are convinced that if only reporters would get these economic facts of life right, the quality of economics coverage would improve immeasurably. In general, these myths fall into four categories of journalistic error:

A Powerful Bias Toward Pessimism

There is an old saying in the media: good news is a contradiction in terms. This seems to be especially true when it comes to coverage of pocketbook issues. Here is just one stark recent example of this pessimistic slant: In late 1999, the Census Bureau reported that incomes for every income group had risen and that the income gap between rich and poor had closed slightly. The Census Bureau researchers called it one of the most upbeat reports on income gains in 15 years, but this stunning report of economic progress received only modest attention from news outlets. A few months later, a left-leaning organization called the Center on Budget and Policy Priorities released a flawed report alleging that the gap between rich and poor was widening. That report, with its pessimistic and erroneous spin, created a national media sensation.

Scientific studies confirm a negative bias in media coverage of the economy. In 1997, the Center for Media and Public Affairs released a study showing that the volume of the news media's economic coverage is highly correlated with the unemployment rate – more joblessness means more TV attention to the economy. Reporting that the GDP is rising and people are able to find jobs with ease is a bit like reporting that no one was murdered downtown today.

Reporters keep revisiting the idea that the future can't possibly be as good as the present or the past. A few years ago, correspondent Harry Smith narrated a prime time CBS News special on the demise of the middle class. "The middle class is shrinking," he told Americans, "and the expectation that our children will be able to live in homes like these, and have lives that are better than our own, is withering." That's nonsense, as Michael Cox demonstrates in Chapter 7, but such a pessimistic bias about our economic environment causes people needless worry about the prospects for their own lives and those of their families.

Excessive pessimism is not coverage of the news; it is distortion of the news. In some cases, biased bad news is presented in a way that promotes the agenda of left-wing activists. Some journalists and interest group spokesmen have said: So what if the data on global warming is debatable? If we get Americans to trim their consumption of fossil fuels, it's a good thing regardless. Others have made this case about counting the homeless. In some cases, reporters conceded that homeless counts were exaggerated, but nonetheless publicized them as a means of motivating public action to help those sleeping on grates. This is not just a blatant violation of journalistic ethics – it also transforms news into propaganda and degrades the journalism profession.

Journalists constantly try to wring the bad news out of a positive story. The joyous birth of the baby who symbolically represented the Earth's six billionth person was portrayed as a frightening tale of a planet infested with excess human beings. "Some say a growing population is the greatest problem facing humanity," fretted CNN's Natalie Pawelski on October 12, 1999. What most reporters failed to highlight was: 1) birth rates are falling drastically all over the world; 2) population growth is a consequence of declining infant mortality and rising life expectancy; 3) per-capita incomes are rising rapidly in most nations all over the world; 4) the doom-and-gloom stories of the past have been contradicted by events; and 5) most advanced nations do not have a *population explosion* problem, but a *population implosion* problem. Birth rates have plummeted to below replacement levels in almost all industrialized nations. In Chapter 5, Nicholas Eberstadt debunks the myth that overpopulation is a dire threat.

One of the world's most respected economic journalists is Michael Prowse of the *Financial Times*. After spending several years in the United States, and on the eve of his return to the U.K., Prowse wrote a brilliant essay about how we Americans uniquely flaunt our vices for the entire world to see. Prowse's observation is worth remembering:

INTRODUCTION

◆

> The U.S. has a much worse reputation than it deserves. Commercial television and cinema present a grotesquely distorted image of modern American life. The tendency of foreigners to bash the U.S. is encouraged by the very openness of the society, which ensures that every possible vice – from political corruption to low school test scores – is paraded before the world.
>
> Other countries try to hide their sins in the interest of progress. Americans take a delight in exposing theirs.

The media are especially guilty of this offense.

An Excessive Reliance On Unreliable Sources

The problem is simply this: There are a lot of very bad economists out there, yet somehow many of them continue to appear regularly in the newspapers and on TV. Perhaps it is because they take pains to ensure they are always accessible to the press, or because they are more "quotable." Consider some recent research by David Hale of Zurich Kemper, which he presents in detail in Chapter 10. Hale found that in the late 1990s blue-chip economic forecasters consistently underestimated the resilience and growth potential of the U.S. economy. The average blue-chip forecast during this period was 2.5 percent, but the actual growth rate of GDP was closer to four percent in real terms. These are gigantic forecasting errors, but no matter how error-prone their track record, the same blundering economists continue to get quoted on TV and in newsprint.

If they're going to do an effective job of informing the public, reporters must do a better job of discovering which experts have been right and which have been wrong. This is especially true when it comes to coverage of fiscal policy. For the past few years, mainstream economists have dismissed reports of budget surpluses as pie-in-the-sky forecasting. Among others, the Urban Institute's Robert Reischauer, a former director of the Congressional Budget Office, has been telling the press for the past four years that the federal tax surpluses are not real; that they are likely to be much smaller than predicted; and that Congress should not count on this money to be there to pay for tax cuts – and in each of the past four years, the forecasts of surpluses have not been too high, but too low.

INTRODUCTION

◆

In January 2000, in a *New York Times* op-ed entitled "The Phantom Surplus," Reischauer wrote that we should "expect [the budget surplus] to be somewhere around $100 billion" – and he was referring to the entire 10-year period from 2000-2010! The recorded surplus for FY2000 alone was well over $200 billion, indicating Reischauer's error rate to be astronomical. Yet despite Reischauer's inaccurate forecasts, he is still routinely quoted in budget and tax stories offering his advice about what the future holds.

It's not just a matter of individual experts with poor track records, either. Relying on statistics collected by the U.S. government, journalists have for years fretted about the "savings crisis" – the ostensible fact that Americans just don't save enough. But as William Gale explains in Chapter 9, there are many economists who argue that standard measures of savings are "arbitrary and increasingly misleading." For example, many investors hold stocks that have greatly increased in value since they were originally purchased, but those unrealized capital gains are excluded from the official figures. "If accrued gains are included," Gale writes, "saving is at its highest level in at least 40 years, not its lowest." Yet many journalists, lacking the sophistication to place the official statistics in their proper context, continue to lecture the public about their failure to save.

In no area is the press guiltier of relying on false experts than with respect to coverage of issues related to the environment, population, resource scarcity, and global food production. The doomsayers' dire predictions have been as wrong as can be over the past 30 years. The air and water are cleaner, life expectancy has risen here and abroad, birth rates are falling, per capita food production has skyrocketed – even as we consume more and grow richer!

One of the gloom industry's leading spokesmen, Lester Brown of the Worldwatch Institute, could hardly have been more wrong when he famously wrote in 1981 that "the period of global food security is over. As the demand for food continues to press against the supply, inevitably, real food prices will rise." Well, no. Real food prices have actually fallen by about one-third to one-half since those words were written. In 1990,

---

Brown – still refusing to acknowledge the error of his ways – wrote in his annual book, *The State of the World*, that "the first concrete evidence of environmental deterioration now seems likely to be rising grain prices." The very next year, grain prices fell by more than 25 percent.

Similarly, Paul Ehrlich was about as wrong as he could have been when he said that the "battle to feed humanity is over. Tens of millions of people will starve to death." The notorious Club of Rome overshot the mark by 300 percent when it predicted $100-a-barrel oil in the year 2000.

But despite this miserable record of accuracy, the media have failed to recognize that the claims of professional doomsayers like Ehrlich and the Worldwatch Institute really belong in supermarket tabloids along with stories of UFOs and Elvis sightings, not in serious newspapers. (In 1969, Ehrlich actually wrote: "I would take even money that England will not exist in the year 2000.") *The State of the World* continues to garner large volumes of media attention for its bleak forecasts. On June 12, 2000 a story in the *Washington Post* was headlined: "Drastic Climate Changes Forecast." The source of the study: the Worldwatch Institute.

Chicken Little may be consistently wrong, but each time he assures us that this time the sky really is falling, gullible editors place his claims on page A-1, above the fold.

Journalists have a duty to report hard truths, but passing along the latest inaccurate theories of those whose past prognostications of gloom have been proven false is the essence of shoddy reporting. Reporters need to conscientiously check the historical record of groups like the Worldwatch Institute. They rarely do.

A Bias in Favor of Government Interventionism

In 1930, before the New Deal, there were fewer than 300 reporters assigned to cover Washington, D.C. By the year 2000, there were more than 10,000 journalists camped out in the capital, all writing about some aspect of the U.S. federal government. It is now second nature for these reporters to ask Washington's bureaucrats and politicians how they would solve economic problems, both real and perceived. The federally-centered press corps automatically regard activist government policies as offering "solutions," and reporters often reward the political sponsors of such policies with good press. But the media frequently denigrate conservatives who believe government is rarely an effective problem-solver, insinuating they somehow lack "compassion" for their "failure" to support more regulations or more federal spending.

Many government programs at the federal level are intended to create jobs and increase American competitiveness. This is often a fiscal illusion. The ability of fiscal policy – particularly government spending – to "stimulate" the economy is a very questionable theory and is often counterproductive in practice, as Milton Friedman shows in Chapter 1. Japan in the 1990s is a good example of the futility of using government spending as a means to boost the economy.

Tax cuts are usually covered in a negative fashion as well. Reporters almost always object to tax cuts as somehow "costing" the government revenue. But as Arthur Laffer and I show in Chapter 3, tax rate cuts can sometimes mean more revenues for the government, not less. A good example is the capital-gains tax cut passed in 1997. Reducing the rate of taxation on income from long-term capital gains from 28 to 20 percent led to a doubling of federal revenues received from this tax – more dollars collected with a lower rate.

One of the great modern success stories in public policy has been airline deregulation. Robert Crandall explains in Chapter 8 that because of deregulation, American travelers now save billions of dollars each year, thanks to substantially lower air fares. But most news stories describe airline deregulation as somehow a burden to consumers. For example, we are often told that airline deregulation has led to a reduction in airline safety. Yet air travel in the 1990s was as safe as it has ever been. Out of the hundreds of thousands of commercial flights in 1998, there was not a single crash. If you took an airline flight every day, you would have to fly for 2,000 years before you would have a greater than 50-50 chance of dying in a crash. The years since airline deregulation have been the safest in aviation history, yet on those rare occasions when a crash does occur, the media are still among the first to raise the question of re-regulation.

Faith in government and wariness of the free market is also a theme when the media cover the economic systems of other nations – especially those that are more socialistic. Noting the anniversary of communism's collapse ten years earlier, CNN's Christiane Amanpour told viewers in November 1999 that "many are saying the unbridled capitalism that followed communism has unleashed misery on citizens who had all their social needs taken care of, especially in the former Soviet Union." When covering Castro's Cuba, the press boast of the superior health care system and better education allegedly found on the socialistic island, as compared with the U.S.

For its part, Americans are often told that Europe offers its workers superior day care, universal health care, job training, job security, and a variety of other benefits denied to U.S. employees. But as William Niskanen documents in Chapter 6, Euro-envy is based on the false premise that workers are prima facie better off as a result of these labor rules. In fact, Europe has a combined unemployment rate nearly twice as high as the U.S., while the Euro has fallen relative to the dollar, and far more capital is now flowing into the U.S. than into Europe.

The tendency within the media – one that is encouraged by outside advocacy groups – is to see every social and economic problem as a clarion call for government action. A 1998 headline on the minimum wage read, "Rise in Minimum Wage Will Mean Pay Raise for 2 Million Low Income Workers." Well, if that were the whole story, who could be against it? The media's failure to routinely explain the deficiencies and unintended consequences of government intervention ranks as one of the greatest sins of omission of our time.

INTRODUCTION

◆

A Failure to Grasp the New Rules of the Information-Age Economy

The new economy is real, but journalists can be excused if they were caught off guard. Most professional economists were, too. The new economy has changed most, if not all, of the old rules. In the past 20 years, our economy has grown by almost 90 percent in real terms. The GDP has averaged a torrid 3.5 percent annual growth rate. We have created some 40 million new jobs, and we now have a shortage of workers, not jobs. The budget deficit has turned into a rapidly rising surplus. Incomes are rising. Inflation is almost nonexistent. The stock market has exploded and so has median family wealth. None of this was ever thought possible – particularly the combination of all this good news.

Yet in the face of this revolutionary progress, the media stubbornly cling to old-economy theories even as these theories are being discredited by events. The Phillips Curve notion that economic growth causes inflation is a non sequitur in the new age economy. Over the past 25 years economic growth and inflation have been negatively, not positively correlated, as Lawrence Kudlow shows in Chapter 2.

In the global information age, the U.S. has imported capital from abroad at record levels. Since the early Reagan years the U.S. has attracted more than $1.5 trillion in net foreign capital. This is because the U.S., with its low inflation and comparatively low tax rates, is the safe harbor for the world's investment capital. Foreigners invest far more in the U.S. than Americans invest abroad. This capital surplus has been a locomotive for the past two decades of U.S. growth. The expanding trade deficit, about which media commentators routinely worry, is actually a signal that we are winning the global race for investment capital. In Chapter 4, Brian Wesbury explains why those monthly trade deficit figures, whose importance has been exaggerated, shouldn't cause journalists to wring their hands.

Two of the clichés most abused by journalists over the past decade have been "the bubble economy" and "the Goldilocks economy." The so-called bubble economy is based on the premise that the stock market is overvalued. These stories have appeared in the media since the Dow Jones was at 5,000. As of this writing, it is approximately 11,000. The economic bubble boys missed the greatest and most rapid market expansion in world history. They failed to envision the potential of the new-age economy. Of course, no one knows whether the market and the economy will continue to climb or sag in the immediate future, but the bubble theorists have been painstakingly wrong for years.

The Goldilocks economy – "it's not too hot and not too cold" – story has also been invalidated. From 1996 to 2000, the economy sizzled at a four percent real growth rate. This is about as hot as it gets for an advanced economy. (A four percent real growth rate translates into the economy doubling in size in less than 20 years.) But here we go again with yet another dysfunctional version of the Phillips Curve theory that growth causes inflation. The experience of the new economy is that the microchip age has so lifted the rate of productivity in America that four to five percent growth is achievable without inflation. There is no such thing as an economy that is "too hot."

Rules For Understanding the New Economy

At the end of each year, the British magazine *The Economist* looks back upon the year just completed to determine what predictions they got right and what they got wrong. The magazine invariably does what very few others do in journalism: they admit when they are wrong. They even try to surmise why they were wrong.

America's economic journalists need a similar period of self-inspection. Their track record of predicting the future direction of the economy has been unimpressive. Their ability to explain the chain reaction of economic events that affect our daily lives has been deficient. Their trust in governmental institutions – from the Federal Reserve to the International Monetary Fund, from the trustbusters at the Justice Department to Congress – to solve economic problems has been excessive. (One example: Most mainstream economic reporters wrote in supportive terms about the IMF bailout of Russia in 1997 and 1998. It was later acknowledged that billions of dollars of the agency's funds were simply stolen by corrupt Russian leaders.)

We would leave reporters with seven simple rules about understanding the new economy:

1) **"Inflation is always and everywhere a monetary phenomenon,"** a simple rule of monetary policy coined by Milton Friedman some 40 years ago, is more true now than ever.

2) **Wages rise with productivity.**

3) **When you tax something, you get less of it; when you tax something less, you get more of it.**

4) **A strong currency is a sign of a strong economy.**

5) **The trade deficit is meaningless.**

6) **Growth is good. (There is no Phillips Curve trade-off between inflation and growth.)**

7) **Markets work: The central planning model is a failure.**

We are convinced the news media can do better in explaining how and why our economy works. We hope the essays that follow will help in that pursuit.

CHAPTER 1

◆

MEDIA MYTH:

Government Spending and Deficits Stimulate the Economy

Milton Friedman

An increase in government spending clearly benefits the individuals who receive the additional spending. Considered by itself, it looks as if the additional spending is a stimulus to the economy.

But that is hardly the end of the story. We have to ask where the government gets the money it spends. The government can get the money in only three ways: increased taxes, borrowing from the public, and creating new money. Let us examine each of these in turn.

Government Spending Financed By Additional Taxation

In this situation, the dollar cost to the persons who pay the taxes is exactly equal to the dollar gain to the persons who receive the spending. It looks like a washout.

Getting the extra taxes, however, requires raising the rate of taxation. As a result, the taxpayer gets to keep less of each dollar earned or received as a return on investment, which reduces his or her incentive to work and to save. The resulting reduction in effort or in savings is a hidden cost of the extra spending. Far from being a stimulus to the economy, extra spending financed through higher taxes is a drag on the economy.

This does not mean that the extra spending can never be justified. However, it can only be justified on the ground that the benefit to the people who receive the spending, or to the community from the activity to be financed by the spending, is greater than the direct harm to the taxpayers plus the hidden cost. It cannot be justified as a way to stimulate the overall economy.

Government Spending Financed By Borrowing From the Public

Individuals who purchase the securities that finance the additional expenditure would have done something else with the money. If they had not purchased the government securities, they presumably would have purchased private securities that would have financed private investment. In other words, government spending crowds out private investment. At this level, it is again a washout: those who receive the extra government spending benefit, but the private investors, who are deprived of the same amount of funds, lose.

But again, that is too simple a story. The overall effect is an increase in the demand for loanable funds, which tends to raise interest rates. The rise in interest rates discourages private demand for funds to make way for the increased government demand. Thus, there is a hidden cost in the form of a lowered stock of productive capital and lower future income.

The Keynesian view that the spending is stimulative assumes that the funds the government borrows would not otherwise have been invested in the private capital market, but came simply from cash held in hoards by individuals – from under the mattress, as it were. In addition, it assumes that there are unemployed resources that can readily be brought into the work force by activating the excess funds held by individuals, without raising prices or wages.

That is a possibility in some special cases, such as the Great Depression in the 1930s, when there had been a major reduction in total output and prices were very far from their equilibrium level. More generally, however, theory suggests and experience confirms that government spending financed by borrowing from the public does not provide a stimulus to the economy.

Figure 1-1

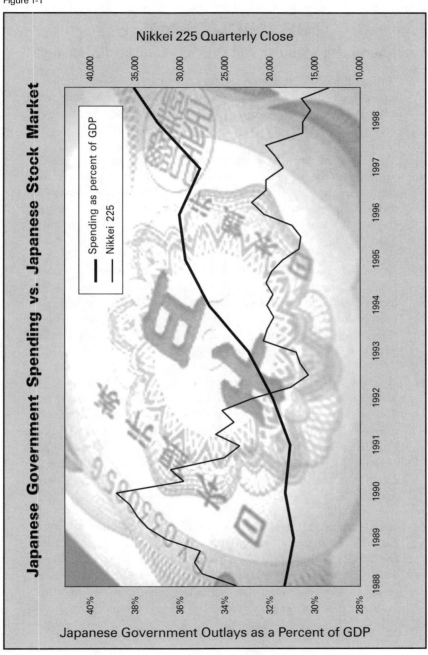

Japanese Government Spending vs. Japanese Stock Market

Nikkei 225 Quarterly Close

Japanese Government Outlays as a Percent of GDP

Spending as percent of GDP
Nikkei 225

THE MEDIA'S MYTH:

Government Spending and Deficits Stimulate the Economy

"I think if Mr. Clinton is elected, he's got to know he's got 100 days to really get the country moving again, and I suspect he will go to some sort of public works program. It did work in the 1930s." – Ray Brady, CBS's *Sunday Morning*, October 25, 1992.

"Despite gradually falling unemployment and a surprising 2.7% surge in the third-quarter gross domestic product, business and consumer spending is expected to continue to languish next year unless Clinton acts to stimulate growth through public works spending or other programs." – John Greenwald, *Time*, November 23, 1992.

"It is deficit spending that stimulates an economy, whether it comes from the private or public sectors. Right now the private sector carries the load. In the next recession, today's cherished budget surpluses must be turned into deficits. The public sector, in effect, must replace at least some of the private sector's deficit spending." – Louis Uchitelle, *New York Times*, August 22, 1999.

"For the first time in modern economic history, fiscal policy is being run the way the textbooks say it should be during good times: The government's big budget surpluses help damp growth and prevent the economy from overheating. The surpluses also give President Clinton and his successors more room to stimulate the economy with spending increases or tax cuts should conditions soften." – Jacob M. Schlesinger and Nicholas Kulish, *Wall Street Journal*, February 1, 2000.

"My guess is that a slowing economy will open minds to a tax cut....What will probably be forgotten in all this is that fiscal stimulus can also result from more government spending. The nation, in my view, will be better served by a more generous earned-income tax credit, to take one example, than by a large tax cut." – Jeff Madrick, "Economic Scene" column, *New York Times*, November 23, 2000.

Japan provides a dramatic recent example. During the 1990s, the Japanese economy was depressed. The government tried repeated fiscal stimulus packages, each involving increases in government spending financed by borrowing. Over the past decade, in fact, Japan has had the largest increase in government spending and government debt of any of the industrialized countries. Yet – or maybe therefore – the Japanese economy has remained depressed. (See Figure 1-1.)

Government Spending Financed By Creating New Money

In this case, there is no first-round private offset to the government spending. It looks as if the public spending is clearly stimulative, and it is. The question is: What is doing the stimulating? Is it the government spending, which in the previous two cases was not stimulative? Or is it the increase in the quantity of money by which the government spending is financed?

Suppose the monetary authorities simply added to the money supply without any change in government spending. (They could do so by purchasing government securities on the market.) The additional demand for government securities would raise their price, which is equivalent to a reduction in the rate of interest. If the sellers of the securities simply put the new money under the mattress, that would end the story and there would be no stimulus. They are far more likely, however, to use the money for some alternative investment, or to spend on consumption. That would lead to exactly the same additional spending as using the money for government spending, but the extra spending would be in the private economy, not the public sector.

Digging deeper, the extra spending will initially be reflected in some combination of increased output and increased prices. The exact division will vary greatly from time to time, depending on the state of the economy, and on whether the extra spending was or was not anticipated. If the initial situation were one of an economy roughly at its capacity level with reasonably full employment, a temporary stimulus to more production would be followed by a higher price level. After the price level had adjusted, the real economy would be back where it had started, unless there were further increases in money, setting off an inflationary spiral.

On the other hand, if the initial position were one of deep recession with unemployed resources, a much larger fraction of the increase in spending would be absorbed by an increase in employment and output, and a much smaller fraction by a rise in prices. Similarly, if the initial situation were one of incipient inflation, even the initial effect might be to produce inflation.

Confusion Between Monetary Stimulus and Fiscal Stimulus

The fallacy that government spending and deficits stimulate the economy has gained credibility because the extra spending is so often financed by creating new money. In that case, fiscal policy (changes in government spending and taxation) and monetary policy (changes in the quantity of money) are both in play and it is easy to attribute the short-term effects of monetary policy to the effects of fiscal policy. In order to get empirical evidence on the separate effects of fiscal and monetary policy, it is necessary to find episodes in which fiscal and monetary policy are moving in opposite directions or one is neutral while the other is not. The example of Japan in the 1990s noted earlier is one such episode. In that case, monetary policy was repressive, or at best neutral, and fiscal stimuli programs were ineffective.

Over the course of years, I have studied a number of similar episodes both in the United States and around the world. In every case, fiscal policy intended to be expansionary was expansionary if and only if monetary policy was accommodating. This empirical evidence is consistent with the theoretical analysis of the preceding sections.

CHAPTER 2

◆

MEDIA MYTH:

Economic Growth Causes Inflation

Lawrence Kudlow

Almost every economics reporter these days was probably exposed to the Phillips Curve at a very young age, probably first during a college or high school economics course. The Phillips Curve indoctrinated a whole generation or two of Americans with the idea that there is a trade-off between economic growth and inflation. The essence of the Phillips Curve logic is that too much growth or too many jobs can spark higher prices; conversely, during times of high joblessness, the federal government can supposedly reduce unemployment by printing more money.

The cousin of the Phillips Curve is the NAIRU, or the Non-Accelerating Inflation Rate of Unemployment. The NAIRU predicts that when growth rates bump up against some predetermined sustainable level, more growth will simply ignite higher levels of inflation. The ideal, under this model, is to constrain economic growth rates to the magical NAIRU rate.

Both theories are dead wrong. The root causes of inflation are excess money and dollar devaluation, not too many people working, producing and prospering.

Reporters' past schooling in the Phillips Curve and NAIRU probably explains why today's media so often report good economic news – higher wages, more jobs created, a faster-than-expected rate of growth – as if it were bad news. They can't seem to shake the notion that the threat of inflation is hovering behind each piece of good economic news. "The latest numbers on the growth of the American economy for the first quarter were very impressive," NBC's Tom Brokaw reported not too long ago before landing the classic undercut: "Maybe too impressive for Wall Street investors, who are worrying about higher interest rates to cool it all off." (*NBC Nightly News,* July 28, 2000.)

During the mid- and late-1990s, we saw one manifestation of the Phillips Curve notion when many economists and reporters talked about the "Goldilocks Economy," meaning an economy that was "not too hot and not too cold, but just right." The idea that an economy can be "too hot" comes right out of the Keynesian Phillips Curve orthodoxy.

A Growing, Productive Economy Does Not Cause Inflation

Is there any validity to the Phillips Curve/NAIRU paradigm? The answer, based on the evidence of the past 30 years, is a resounding "no." Growth does not cause inflation; if anything, it is the absence of growth and output that causes prices to rise. As economist Arthur Laffer explains, "When the economy produces more apples, the price of apples should fall, not rise." Similarly, higher wages are not inflationary if they are driven by productivity increases, as they have been throughout most of the past two decades in the U.S.

For the same reason, falling unemployment has in no way been associated with higher inflation, as the NAIRU adherents believe. Figure 2-1 shows that just the opposite has been true. In the 1970s, for example, both inflation and unemployment steadily rose together. By the early 1980s, inflation had hit 11 percent and unemployment topped out at eight percent. In fact, the creed of the Phillips Curve actually contributed to the stagflation, as officials used inflationary monetary policy to try to stimulate real economic growth rates and thus achieve a decline in unemployment. The lesson learned was that printing more money doesn't generate more jobs – in fact, in this case, the inflation outburst so destabilized the economy that jobs were lost in record numbers.

As Figure 2-1 also shows, since the early 1980s inflation and unemployment have been in a long-term decline – and both statistics

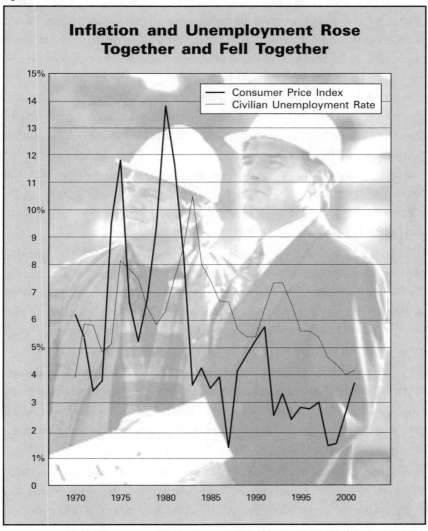

Figure 2-1

Inflation and Unemployment Rose Together and Fell Together

- Consumer Price Index
- Civilian Unemployment Rate

have fallen together. The inflation rate has fallen by 10 percentage points, the unemployment rate by nearly five percentage points. Again, the Phillips Curve logic would have predicted the opposite effect. The decline of one of these economic variables should have caused the other to rise.

CHAPTER 2

◆

By the 1990s, the Phillips Curve was so discredited by the actual events of the previous two decades that it gave way to the more economically sophisticated NAIRU argument: too much growth is too much of a good thing. NAIRU's adherents thought the prudent course for the Fed and Congress would be to try to hold the economic growth rate down to 2.5 percent or so to avoid more inflation. This, of course, ignores actual economic history. Since 1947, real economic growth in the U.S. averaged 3.5 percent annually. But in the 1990s, NAIRU broke down as well. The growth rate in 1997 and 1998 rose to four percent in real terms, but inflation did not show any signs of flaring up. In fact, the concern in those years was *deflation*. Spurred by the technology revolution, economic growth between 1994 and 2000 registered 4.9 percent annually with only 1.8 percent inflation.

In 1999 and 2000, the real economic growth rate hit nearly five percent, and yet inflation was still under control. This also contradicts the NAIRU concept. The "Goldilocks" economy paradigm that had been in vogue just a few years earlier now appeared foolish. After all, if five percent growth rates weren't inciting inflation, how "hot" would the economy have to get before it got too hot?

We should have learned from the experience of the past several years in particular that high rates of economic growth – in the four to five percent range – are sustainable without inciting inflation. We also should have learned that an unemployment rate below four percent is not necessarily inflationary.

How can this be? The short answer is that low inflation causes growth, or at least nurtures it. We need to go back to elementary economics. We were all taught (or we should have been taught) that "inflation is too many dollars chasing too few goods." If the value of money is held constant, the production of more goods actually reduces prices.

In recent years even the Phillips Curve/NAIRU proponents have revised their earlier guesstimates about how much growth the economy could sustain without causing price increases. Those who once thought that the growth rate of the economy could not rise above 2.5 percent now say that the NAIRU growth rate is closer to 3.5 to four percent.

THE MEDIA'S MYTH:
Economic Growth Causes Inflation

"Investors are betting that a chill wind from Asia will cool off this superheated economy and relieve inflationary pressures that could surface in 1998....Unemployment is now clearly below nearly all estimates of the economy's 'full employment' rate. That level is generally pegged anywhere from 5% to 6%. A jobless rate below that point means that labor demand is outstripping supply, which is why wage growth has sped up noticeably. – James C. Cooper & Kathleen Madigan, *Business Week*, December 22, 1997.

"Is the good news getting too good? The economy continues to roar, but there are more and more signs that it's on the verge of overheating. Because of mounting fears of inflation, long-term interest rates advanced to just under 6 percent last week – a level that hasn't been breached in over a year." – Jack Egan, "Nothing Good Lasts Forever," *U.S. News & World Report*, June 14, 1999.

"As President Clinton declared to thunderous applause last week, the state of the union is the strongest it's ever been. Maybe it's even too much of a good thing. At least the sizzling growth rate of the final quarter of last year is setting off smoke alarms that the economy may be overheating and raising the threat of inflation." – George Watson, ABC's *World News Now*, February 1, 2000.

"It may be months or years before it will be possible to judge whether Mr. Greenspan is doing the right thing for the right reasons. Some economists think the Fed chairman is taking a straightforward situation – an economy that is growing too fast for its own good – and overanalyzing the causes." – Richard W. Stevenson, "Pondering Greenspan's Next Moves," *New York Times*, March 20, 2000.

"The Federal Reserve, which has worried that a red-hot economy was growing too fast and could spark higher inflation, raised interest rates six times from June 1999 through May of this year to cool it down." – Glenn Kessler, "White House Mocks Cheney on Economy," *Washington Post*, December 5, 2000.

But no law of nature says economies can't grow at a rate faster than four percent. What the NAIRU crowd, and too many in the press who listen to them, still haven't internalized is that the reality of the new information age means economic growth rates can be sustained at much higher levels than previously believed. The high-technology revolution is powerfully raising productivity rates of American workers and industries.

In effect, technology breakthroughs and productivity gains act on the economy like tax cuts, raising economic growth and lowering inflation. Growth rates of five or six percent or even more are achievable, and the economic record of the late 1990s bears this out. These growth rates are especially sustainable if policymakers simultaneously enact policies that increase investment and savings, such as supply-side tax cuts.

Inflation Can't Be Used to Create Wealth, Either

One final point: Monetary policy cannot be used as a tool to increase growth and should not be used as a tool to slow growth. The objective of a sound monetary policy is to achieve price stability. The eradication of inflation has spurred the most prolonged capital investment boom and the greatest build-up in real wealth in world history, with asset prices rising by an estimated $10 trillion. With the economy showing signs of slowing down at the time of this writing (November 2000), it is extremely illogical to argue that more inflation can produce growth or end the slump in the stock market.

Since a zero inflation regime (correctly measured) is optimal, any deviation from zero inflation is economically suboptimal. If printing money could cause economic growth, then Russia and Argentina would be very wealthy nations today.

Economic reporters should abandon their devotion to Phillips Curve logic when covering the economy and the stock market. The Alice in Wonderland logic that growth is bad and unemployment increases are good has the public perplexed, as it should be. With the right configuration of growth-oriented policies – namely, lower tax rates, sound money, free trade, and deregulation – the potential of the economy to create rising levels of prosperity in this information age seems almost limitless.

CHAPTER 3

◆

MEDIA MYTH:

Tax Cuts Always Cause a Loss of Revenue

Arthur Laffer and *Stephen Moore*

When covering tax policy, the media often fall into one of three traps. First, they usually portray tax reductions as fiscally irresponsible, because they anticipate that the federal government will suffer a loss of revenue. Many journalists still insist, erroneously, that the so-called "voodoo" tax cuts enacted by Ronald Reagan contributed to large budget deficits.

Second, the media seldom acknowledge that tax rate reductions can, and often do, affect the economic behavior of workers, investors, and firms, thereby improving economic efficiency. That is to say, the press is guilty of the fallacy of static economic forecasting.

And finally, the media often parrot the reflexive claims of liberal-leaning organizations that every tax reduction policy will disproportionately benefit the wealthy.

Tax Policy: The Theory Behind the Supply Side Model

The core of the problem is that the press and many policy analysts treat all tax cuts alike. They fail to distinguish between *demand-side tax cuts*, which are oriented toward putting more money into people's pockets in order to spur consumer spending, and *supply-side tax cuts*, which are crafted to encourage economically productive activities such as working, saving, investing, and risk taking. Taxes matter at the margin, so incentive-based tax reductions emphasize cutting high tax rates to reduce the distortionary impact of tax policy.

Figure 3-1

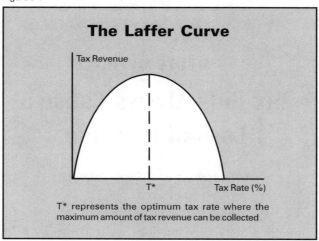

The Laffer Curve

Tax Revenue

T*   Tax Rate (%)

T* represents the optimum tax rate where the
maximum amount of tax revenue can be collected

The Laffer curve provides a framework for understanding the potential impact of tax-rate changes on economic behavior. As Figure 3-1 shows, there are two tax rates that will produce zero revenue for the government. The first, of course, is a tax rate of zero. The second is a tax rate of 100 percent. That's because if the government were to take every penny of earnings, no one would work. (Actually, people would work, but they would not report the income to the tax collector and so the government would get close to nothing.)

The Laffer curve illustrates two points. First, for every amount of tax raised, there are two tax rates. It is always economically inefficient to impose a tax rate that is higher than the revenue-maximizing tax rate. The second illustrative point of the Laffer curve is that cutting tax rates will increase economic output because the disincentive to work and save and invest is lowered as tax rates are raised. The higher the initial tax rate, the stronger the supply-side effect of lowering that rate.

Here is a simple way to measure the impact of a tax: Start by subtracting the tax rate from 1.00. A tax rate of 80 percent, for example, allows the individual to keep 20 cents for every dollar earned. If that rate is lowered to 60 percent, the incentive to work is doubled, because the worker now keeps 40 cents for every dollar earned. As tax rates fall, the positive impact of continuing to lower rates is diminished. Thus, if the starting tax rate is 40 percent, the worker or investor keeps 60 cents on the dollar. Lowering the tax rate to 20 percent increases the return to 80 cents.

In both of those examples, the tax rate was reduced by 20 percentage points, but in the first case, the incentive to work and invest was doubled, whereas in the second case the incentive to work and invest rose by only one third.

If we accept the premise that people work, save, and invest to earn money, then it stands to reason that increasing the rewards of working, saving and investing will lead to more of it, while taxing away those rewards will lead to less of it. As Supreme Court Chief Justice John Marshall famously wrote in the landmark *McCulloch v. Maryland* decision, "The power to tax is the power to destroy."

It is an iron law of economics that when you tax something, you get less of it; when you tax something less, you get more of it. We tax bad things like cigarettes because we want to discourage people from smoking. But we also tax behavior that is virtuous – working, saving, and investing – and so we get less of that than we would without taxes.

Income Tax Rates: The Historical Evidence

There is solid empirical evidence which validates the Laffer curve, starting with the three episodes of significant tax reduction in the United States during the 20th century. The first of these cuts occurred in the 1920s, under Presidents Warren Harding and Calvin Coolidge; the second in the 1960s, under President John F. Kennedy; the last, in the 1980s, under President Ronald Reagan. In all three cases, critics warned that rate reductions would lead to declining government revenues, but federal revenues increased after each cut in tax rates.

The Harding-Coolidge tax cuts reduced the top income-tax rate in stages from the World War I high of 73 percent down to 25 percent in 1925. This was a very large and unprecedented reduction in rates on the

---

wealthy. President Coolidge argued for the reductions in his 1924 State of the Union address by reminding the public that "when the taxation of large incomes is excessive they tend to disappear." He confidently predicted that his plan "would actually yield more revenues to the government if the basis of taxation were scientifically revised downward."

Figure 3-2

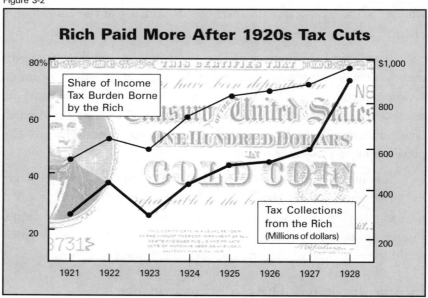

Figure 3-2: **Rich Paid More After 1920s Tax Cuts**

Share of Income Tax Burden Borne by the Rich

Tax Collections from the Rich (Millions of dollars)

Based on the type of static revenue analysis that the Congressional Budget Office uses today to predict the revenue impact of tax-rate reductions, one would have expected a huge depletion of tax collections, but just the opposite occurred. Total tax revenues rose from $720 million in 1921 to $1.15 billion in 1928 as economic growth surged.

Additionally, as Figure 3-2 shows, more of the money flowing to Washington came from the wealthiest Americans, even as their tax rates were being chopped by two-thirds. The share of taxes paid by those earning over $50,000 (the rich back then) rose from 45 percent in 1921, when the top rate was 73 percent, to 62 percent in 1925, when the top rate was 25 percent.

THE MEDIA'S MYTH:
Tax Cuts Always Cause a Loss of Revenue

"Unfortunately, when the supply-side doctrine was tested in the early 1980s, the Treasury Department lost $644 billion in forgone revenues, the federal debt doubled in size and there was no special burst of worker productivity or investment activity." – David Hage and Robert F. Black, "The repackaging of Reaganomics," *U.S. News & World Report*, December 12, 1994.

"[Dole's] proposed tax cuts are so enormous – $551 billion over six years, according to the nonpartisan Joint Tax Committee – as to leave him wide open to charges they will cause the federal deficit to balloon....A case could be made that the candidate who best represents the fiscally conservative, moderate Republican tradition is, believe it or not, Bill Clinton." – George J. Church, "Calculating Dole: 15% or Bust," *Time*, August 19, 1996.

"Bush's tax plan is even more expensive than the Republican tax cut President Clinton vetoed last summer....The Congressional Budget Office projects total surpluses of only $463 billion over the first five years of Bush's plan, but his tax cut alone would cost $483 billion, leaving no money for higher defense or education spending." – David Bloom, *NBC Nightly News*, December 1, 1999.

"Analysts say these candidates must know this, that the country can't really afford these kinds of tax cuts or these kinds of tax credits." – Stacey Tisdale, CBS's *Saturday Early Show*, March 4, 2000.

"On Capitol Hill, the heads of appropriations committees can already be heard complaining that Congress might have to impose budget ceilings in the spring to help pay for the tax cut. Such spending cuts – for example, in key areas like housing, transportation, and the environment – would make it clearer than ever that the Bush tax-cut proposals are too costly because they use up the federal surpluses for a giveaway to the wealthy." – "Tax-Cut News for Mr. Bush," *New York Times* (editorial), February 20, 2001.

In the 1960s, the Kennedy tax cuts provided the same salutary effects. "It is a paradoxical truth," the President proclaimed in 1962 in recommendation of his tax-cut program, "that tax rates are too high today, and tax revenues are too low and the soundest way to raise the revenues in the long run is to cut the tax rates."

President Kennedy was right. "The unusual budget spectacle of sharply rising revenues following the biggest tax cut in history," announced a 1966 *U.S. News and World Report* article, "is beginning to astonish even those who pushed hardest for tax cuts in the first place." Indeed, after the tax cuts took effect, federal tax collections rose from $107 billion in 1963 to $153 billion in 1968. This shocked almost all observers, but even more shocking was the impact on the distribution of taxes paid. Figure 3-3 demonstrates that wealthy individuals paid a much greater share of the nation's tax burden after their rates were lowered. Americans earning over $50,000 per year (the equivalent of about $200,000 today) paid

Figure 3-3

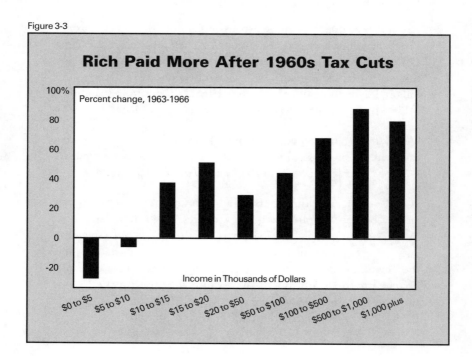

◆

the U.S. Treasury nearly 40 percent more money after rates were cut; their tax share rose from 12 percent of the total in 1963 to almost 15 percent in 1966.

The Lesson of the Reagan Tax Cuts

In 1981, President Reagan proposed and signed into law a 25 percent across-the-board tax-rate reduction plan that was modeled after President Kennedy's successful tax cut from twenty years earlier. Not surprisingly, it produced the same very positive results. Tax revenues grew by $52 billion per year in the 1980s after rates were cut, versus just $35 billion per year in the 1970s. Once again, despite lower tax rates, the rich paid a larger share of the total. In fact, as Figure 3-4 shows, the top one percent paid 17.6 percent of all taxes when the top rate was 70 percent in 1981, but 27.5 percent in 1988 when the rate hit its low of 28 percent. The super-rich, the top one-tenth of one percent of income earners, saw their

Figure 3-4

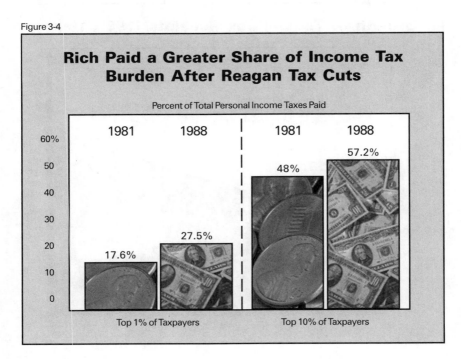

Rich Paid a Greater Share of Income Tax Burden After Reagan Tax Cuts

Percent of Total Personal Income Taxes Paid

| | 1981 | 1988 | 1981 | 1988 |

60%
50
40
30
20
10
0

1981: 17.6% 1988: 27.5% — Top 1% of Taxpayers
1981: 48% 1988: 57.2% — Top 10% of Taxpayers

share of income taxes paid double from seven percent to 14 percent. A study by Harvard economist Lawrence Lindsey, now an economic advisor to President George W. Bush, conclusively proved that the government "collected more revenue from upper-income taxpayers at a 50 percent top rate than it would have at 70 percent."

One of the greatest media myths of all time is that the Reagan tax cut caused the budget deficits of the 1980s, but it's just that – a media myth. From 1980 through 1990, federal tax receipts grew seven percent annually, doubling from $517 billion to $1,035 billion, as shown in Figure 3-5.

As David Rosenbaum, one of the few reporters to see past the partisan smoke-and-mirrors, noted in the *New York Times* in 1992: "One popular misconception is that the Republican tax cuts caused the crippling federal

Figure 3-5

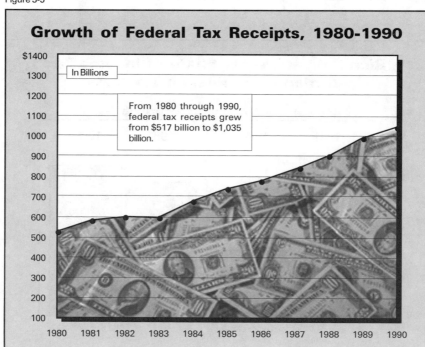

Growth of Federal Tax Receipts, 1980-1990

In Billions

From 1980 through 1990, federal tax receipts grew from $517 billion to $1,035 billion.

budget deficit now approaching $300 billion a year. The fact is, the large deficit resulted because the government vastly expanded what it spent each year...."

In the 1990s, of course, tax policy moved in the opposite direction. In 1990, Congress wanted the rich to pay more taxes, so then-President George H. W. Bush agree to raise the top tax rate on the wealthy from 28 to 31 percent. In an article entitled "Oops! Weren't We Going to Soak the Rich?," the *Wall Street Journal* reported that income tax collections in 1991 from those earning in excess of $200,000 actually declined by $6.5 billion, even as income taxes paid by everyone else rose by $3 billion. Harvard economist Robert Barro wrote that the share of taxes paid by the rich declined from 22 percent in the late 1980s, after Reagan cut tax rates, to 20 percent in 1991 after Bush raised them. In other words, Congress tried to soak the rich with higher tax rates, but it was the middle class that got all wet.

In 1993, President Clinton raised tax rates from 33 percent to 39.6 percent. That tax hike ended up gaining revenues for the federal government, a fact which would seem to contradict the notion that increasing tax rates is economically harmful. But in the 1990s, the adverse impact of the tax hikes was more than neutralized by the positive effects of declining inflation rates, the enactment of two free trade agreements (NAFTA and GATT) that acted as huge tax cuts on trade, and a late 1990s supply-side capital-gains tax cut. Thanks to the retreat in inflation, real tax rates were not much higher in the late 1990s than they were in the early 1990s.

Thus, in each of the three cases of income tax rate reductions in the 20th century, we saw three effects:

1) Total tax revenues rose.

2) Tax payments and the tax share paid by the wealthy increased.

3) The rate of economic growth increased.

CHAPTER 3

◆

The Capital Gains Story

The most vivid example of the Laffer curve in action is the story of changes in capital gains taxation. For nearly 40 years, every time Congress has raised the tax on capital gains, revenues from this tax have declined. Every time the rate has been reduced, revenues have surged. Every time.

Consider the most recent capital-gains tax cut, enacted in 1997. According to Treasury Department tax collection data, in 1996, the year before the long-term capital-gains tax rate was sliced from 28 to 20 percent, the total net capital gains on assets sold was $260 billion. A year later, capital gains had mysteriously jumped to $400 billion. (The capital gains tax cut was retroactive to May of 1997.) In 1998, the total was $450 billion. In 1999, total capital gains exceeded $500 billion.

The Treasury Department data also indicate that the government's revenues from taxation of capital gains have similarly exploded. In 1996, the last year with the 28 percent rate, the government collected $62 billion in capital gains receipts. Table 3-1 shows what happened next:

Table 3-1

Capital Gains: Lower Rates, More Revenues

Year	Tax Rate	Capital Gains Taxes
1996	28%	$62 billion
1997	20%	$79 billion
1998	20%	$89 billion
1999	20%	$109 billion

Seldom in economics does real life so decisively confirm theory: Lower tax rates changed people's economic behavior, stimulated economic growth, and therefore created more, not less, tax revenues.

This was not a one-time aberration. After the capital-gains rate was cut from 28 to 20 percent in 1981, the government's revenues from this tax leapt from $12.5 billion in 1980 to $18.5 billion by 1983 – a 48 percent increase. More importantly, slashing the income and capital-gains tax rates in 1981 helped launch what we now recognize as the greatest and longest period of wealth creation in world history. In 1981, the stock market was cratered at about 1,000, compared to approximately 11,000 today.

MEDIA MYTH: TAX CUTS ALWAYS CAUSE A LOSS OF REVENUE

CHAPTER 3

◆

Conversely, the perverse action in 1986 of raising the capital-gains tax caused total asset sales of taxable capital gains to evaporate, from $326 billion in 1986 (the year before the rate was raised back to 28 percent) to $154 billion in 1989.

How is it that lower capital-gains tax rate lead to more revenues? The capital-gains tax is a voluntary and thus an easily avoided tax. When the tax rate is high, investors simply delay selling their assets – stocks, properties, businesses, etc. – to keep the tax collector away from their door. When the capital-gains tax is cut, asset holders are inspired to sell. Moreover, because a lower capital-gains tax substantially lowers the cost of capital, it encourages risk-taking and causes the economy to grow faster, thereby raising all government receipts in the long term.

So the torrent of new revenues into the government coffers is really no mystery at all. In fact, it was entirely predictable. So then why did so few predict it? The answer is that the government's forecasting models are flawed. Table 3-2 shows that actual capital-gains realizations and tax revenues are far, far higher than forecasted. Much of the increase was attributable to the sizzling stock market in the late 1990s, but a lower capital gains cut increases the after-tax return on capital and thus helps create the strong market. (Hint: One sure way to pump new life into the NASDAQ is to cut the capital-gains tax to 15 percent.)

Table 3-2

Actual Receipts Far Exceeded Pre-Tax Estimate

(Billions of Dollars)

Net Capital Gains	1997	1998	1999
Jan. 1997 Estimate	205	215	228
Actual	384	450	505

Taxes on Gains	1997	1998	1999
Jan. 1997 Estimate	55	65	75
Actual	79	89	109

The critics were famously wrong in their predictions about the fiscal impact of a supply-side capital-gains tax cut. Michael Kinsley of *Slate* magazine, among others, wrote that a capital-gains cut would reduce federal revenues by $75 billion over five years. Instead, the rate cut is on pace to have raised capital gains revenues by $100 billion. What accounts for such a giant forecasting error? These journalistic critics refuse to consider dynamic revenue forecasts, and so they fail to take into account the economic adrenaline that a capital-gains tax cut provides.

Lest there be any confusion, however, the logic behind cutting the capital-gains tax is not to maximize revenues for the government, but to maximize private wealth creation. That probably occurs at a capital gains rate of zero. A capital-gains tax is merely a punitive second layer of tax: the value of a capital asset is no more nor less than the discounted present value of the revenue stream it produces. Under a rational tax system, we would tax either the income stream or the asset value, but not both. Now, assuming we had no tax on capital gains, the revenues would fall to zero. But by ending the double tax on investment, the economy would produce more risk-taking, more productivity, higher wages, and a rise in corporate profits.

Throw Out Static Models

The impact of tax changes cannot be properly predicted without assessing how the tax-policy changes will influence the behavior of workers, entrepreneurs, and investors. All over the world, tax rates are falling as political leaders realize that high tax rates do not redistribute income, they redistribute people. The static economic model used by the Joint Tax Committee and the Congressional Budget Office should be discarded because it has proven again and again that it has no predictive powers. Just as importantly, reporters must stop relying on static analysis if they hope to understand and communicate the likely impact of tax policy changes.

CHAPTER 4

◆

MEDIA MYTH:

Trade Deficits Are Bad News For the U.S. Economy

Brian Wesbury

For most of the 1980s, the popular press was filled with references to an arcane economic theory. This theory explained that the federal budget deficit caused the foreign trade deficit. Conventional wisdom referred to these two deficits as "twins."

According to the "twin deficit" theory, the budget deficit drained savings from the United States and pushed up interest rates. Higher interest rates drove up the value of the dollar and caused the United States to depend on foreign investment. These forces created the trade deficit. Many called for tax increases, protectionism, or devaluation to ward off the coming economic crisis caused by the evil twins.

While the "twin deficit" theory became a popular attack on the Reagan Administration, many economists argued strenuously against it. These economists believed that the trade deficit was caused by an investment surplus. They argued that in a world with floating exchange rates, trade accounts must balance. Every dollar spent overseas must come back to the United States in the form of purchases or investment (i.e., the trade deficit must equal the capital surplus). And in the 1980s, because the United States was an attractive place to invest, the inflow of foreign capital created a trade deficit.

Most of these economists were supply-siders, including Bob Bartley, Bruce Bartlett, George Gilder, Larry Kudlow, Arthur Laffer, Larry Lindsey, Alan Reynolds, and others. While conventional wisdom mocked them, they proved to be right.

Just one twin is alive today. In the third quarter of 2000, despite a federal budget surplus of $237 billion in FY2000, the United States trade deficit hit a record annualized level of $373 billion, or 3.7 percent of GDP. While the federal budget is moving toward bigger surpluses, the trade deficit is growing larger.

Also bucking the conventional wisdom are Germany and Japan. Both of these countries have large federal budget deficits, but their trade accounts are in surplus. Both economies are performing miserably and capital is flowing away from them and toward the United States.

Obviously, something is wrong with the traditional and popular theories about budget and trade deficits. Nonetheless, the trade deficit is still feared by many and instead of rethinking their arguments, those who believed in the twin deficits now blame the lack of private saving for the expanding trade deficit.

According to this new theory, United States consumers save too little and spend too much. This causes imports to grow and forces foreigners to finance our deficit. Eventually, according to this new theory, the dollar and the economy will collapse when foreigners grow tired of financing our "unsustainable" lack of savings.

Conventional Wisdom Is Wrong Again

The twin views, that either a lack of government saving or a lack of private saving causes the trade deficit, are similar, but equally wrong. The savings rate does not determine whether or not an economy has a trade surplus or deficit. Trade deficits are caused by the relative strength of an economy and the attractiveness of investment in that economy.

One look at the chart below and the mistake becomes clear. Figure 4-1 shows the trade deficit plotted against the sum of personal savings and the federal government surplus. As can be seen, the total of federal and personal savings has risen dramatically since 1992 as the budget surplus emerged, but the trade deficit grew to record size.

It is not the amount of domestic savings that determines the trade deficit, but instead the opportunities available for investment. In an

Figure 4-1

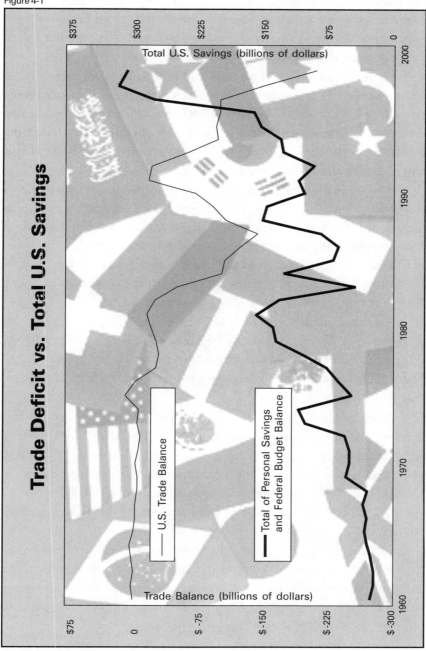

Figure 4-1

Trade Deficit vs. Total U.S. Savings

Total U.S. Savings (billions of dollars)

U.S. Trade Balance

Total of Personal Savings
and Federal Budget Balance

Trade Balance (billions of dollars)

economy with no investment opportunities, there would be no need for domestic or foreign savings. On the other hand, in an economy with great opportunities, domestic and foreign savings will expand until all of the opportunities are funded.

Countries that have lower taxes and less-regulated markets tend to be more attractive places to start businesses, and therefore are also more attractive places to invest. And since 1982, the United States has created a fabulous environment for investment by cutting taxes, loosening regulations, and slowing the growth in government spending. This is why the trade deficit has expanded.

The United States has grown faster than the rest of the world in recent years and three things have occurred. First, as returns on capital increased, foreigners boosted their demand for investments. Second, in order to obtain the purchasing power to make those investments, foreigners needed to sell more goods and services to Americans than they bought from them. Third, a strong domestic economy increased imports by raising the purchasing power of American consumers.

The trade deficit actually indicates strength in an economy, not weakness. The 18-year boom that began in 1982 is being driven by the most rapid increases in productivity ever seen in the history of the United States. This boom requires massive investment and it is that investment that is pulling in foreign funds.

Many analysts wait on pins and needles for foreigners to sell their investments, but the only reason to sell would be if the United States reverses the policy decisions that brought it to this point. By raising taxes, increasing regulation, and expanding the size of government, the United States could make investment less attractive. But until that occurs, America will remain an attractive place to invest and the trade deficit will continue to exist.

During the past five years, the United States economy has grown almost twice as fast as the European Union and nearly four times as fast as Japan. The strong dollar has not stopped foreign investors from investing in the United States. Potential returns from the high-tech boom have attracted investment from all corners of the world.

CHAPTER 4

◆

Individuals Trade, Not Countries

Viewing the trade deficit as if it emanated from a country and not individuals is another major mistake. For example, the trade deficit is not with Japan, but with individual Japanese citizens and businesses. Individuals make billions of decisions every day and in a world with low tariffs and free trade, some of those decisions involve foreign trade or investment. It is individuals that create trade deficits, not countries.

Directed by an invisible hand, consumers and businesses make decisions every day, based on price and quality, potential return, and risk. These decisions may result in a trade deficit or a trade surplus, even though each individual acts in his own self interest.

Any attempt to determine whether this is good or bad is moot.

If the underlying conditions change, then consumers and businesses will alter their decisions. For example, in today's global economy, differing tax rates, wage rates, and productivity have forced the world's production base to spread out. Goods are now being produced in the lowest-cost areas of the world and then shipped back to higher-cost areas.

To a large extent, the trade deficit reflects this global phenomenon. As much as 35 percent of imports come from U.S. companies that produce overseas and then import back home. Foreign companies also produce in the United States and then ship elsewhere. As a result, much of the trade deficit is illusory. A slight shift in production costs or potential returns anywhere in the world can move the trade deficit rapidly.

By cutting costs, companies benefit from the global economy. But consumers also benefit. Increased competition from imports and overseas production holds down prices and increases quality and, as long as the United States economy grows faster than other economies, consumer demand will increase and imports will remain strong. This is why the trade deficit shrinks during recessions and increases during booms.

In 1980 and again in 1991, when the economy was in recession, the trade gap virtually disappeared. Yet, when the economy was booming between 1982 and 1987, and again between 1992 and 2000, the trade deficit expanded.

In boom times, not only do consumers buy more imports, but foreign businesses make more investments in the United States. When the economy slows, these decisions are reversed.

A trade deficit often reflects a strong economy, while a trade surplus can signal a weak one.

Trade and Globalization

Despite the fact that most economists support free trade, there is a growing resentment toward globalization. Violent protests have taken place at virtually every major gathering of international economic leaders in recent years and globalization is blamed for a plethora of perceived economic problems.

Labor unions, one of the most vocal of all anti-free-traders, argue that the United States trade deficit reflects a lack of competitiveness in the United States and that the trade deficit costs jobs. These are hard arguments to support given current economic data.

The unemployment rate fell to 3.9 percent in 2000, its lowest level in over 30 years. Also in 2000, exports grew by nearly 15 percent. Moreover, during the past eight years, exports grew at an average rate of 7.9 percent, two percent faster than the 5.9 percent growth rate of GDP.

If the United States had lost its competitiveness, exports would be growing slower than GDP, and if imports were causing a loss of jobs, unemployment would be on the rise. More importantly, if the United States were not competitive, foreign investment would not be flooding in.

From Bad to Worse

Those who are concerned about the trade deficit ignore these arguments and make an assumption that any kind of "deficit" is a bad thing. This may be human nature; the word "deficit" sounds bad. But the policies that would fix a trade deficit are even worse.

There are three main policy tools typically prescribed to fix a trade deficit: trade protectionism, tax hikes, and currency devaluation. Each of these has side effects that do horrible damage to an economy.

CHAPTER 4

◆

Trade protectionism, like the Smoot-Hawley Tariff Act of 1930, damages an economy by interfering with the efficient allocation of capital. Trade occurs between individuals because each benefits. Cutting off these benefits is, by definition, harmful to the economy. This is especially true as globalization occurs in the information age.

Information is climbing in value relative to real assets and production is shifting rapidly to the lowest-cost areas of the world. Any attempt to interfere with this allocation of capital by enacting protectionist laws would have detrimental effects on the world economy.

Tax hikes, another proposed fix, would slow the economy, lower consumption, and reduce imports. At the same time, tax hikes would reduce the incentive for foreigners to invest and reduce the inflow of capital.

In Europe, high tax rates reduce growth, raise unemployment, and cause capital flight. This is one of the main reasons European countries are running trade surpluses.

Finally, currency devaluation has been used in the past to fix trade deficits, but it has always caused harmful collateral damage. Devaluation makes imports more expensive, while exports become cheap. However, currency devaluation also causes inflation. This inflation drives up interest rates and erodes consumer purchasing power.

Devaluation reduces living standards and economic growth, while increasing inflation. Slow growth and inflation equals stagflation, and stagflation is an excessively high price to pay in order to eliminate a benign trade deficit.

Just Look At History

During the 19th century, the United States became the largest and most productive economy on the face of the Earth. Starting from virtually nothing, America surpassed the great empires of Europe in productivity, living standards, and wealth creation. This occurred despite a number of wars and many economic crises along the way.

THE MEDIA'S MYTH:
Trade Deficits Are Bad News for the U.S. Economy

"For months, what some analysts call the 'twin towers' – the huge, stubborn U.S. trade deficit and the federal government's budget deficit – have cast a shadow over the nation's financial markets." – John M. Berry, "Nation's Twin Deficits Finally Taking a Toll," *Washington Post*, October 20, 1987.

"The trade deficit in January set a new record: a colossal $17 billion. Cheap imports put downward pressure on the price of American goods – to which the rest of the world responds by cutting their prices even more. At some point, the United States will have all the Monopoly money and all the hotels on Boardwalk and Park Place, and everyone else will be out of the game." – Howard Fineman, "In the Line of Fire," *Newsweek*, March 29, 1999.

"The insatiable American appetite for German cars, French perfume and Japanese televisions has helped the world's wealthiest countries grow faster than at any time since the mid-1990s, but the United States is warning that its allies need to join in the gluttony....The United States trade deficit has been a persistent concern for years, of course. But American policymakers are frustrated by its stubbornness during a period of relative prosperity abroad." – Joseph Kahn, "Trade Deficit Set Record in November," *New York Times*, January 21, 2000.

"On the CBS MarketWatch, the downside of the booming U.S. economy. Americans bought so many foreign products last year, it drove the trade deficit up 50 percent to a record $339 billion." – Bob Schieffer, *CBS Evening News*, March 15, 2000.

"The warning signs are clear. Americans depend so heavily on imports that they spend $1 billion a day more buying from abroad than they earn by selling goods overseas. It's the largest trade deficit relative to the overall economy in recent history. Global investors will sooner or later decide they can do better by putting their money in other countries. That would undercut the value of the dollar, make imports more expensive, and fuel inflation even as the economy slows." – Joseph Kahn, "Now, 3 Bears: Weak Dollar, Trade Gap and Inflation," *New York Times*, January 14, 2001.

CHAPTER 4

◆

For 78 out of the 110 years between 1790 and 1900, the United States ran trade deficits with the rest of the world. America imported capital to build railroads and factories, and these investments created the greatest economy on earth.

The same thing is happening today. The United States is building a new empire and making massive investments in the information age. This investment requires the importation of foreign capital and this results in a trade deficit. At the same time, the global economy is becoming a reality. Worldwide, imports and exports are expanding faster than world GDP.

Those countries leading the surge toward the information age are running trade deficits; those falling behind are running trade surpluses. Attempts by government to turn a trade deficit into a trade surplus almost always do more economic harm than good.

CHAPTER 5

◆

MEDIA MYTH:

Too Many People,
Too Few Natural Resources

Nicholas Eberstadt

For many decades – and since the 1971 publication of the Club of Rome's famous doomsday report, *Limits to Growth* – the media have regularly depicted global population growth as a problem, or even an outright crisis: a tendency propelling humanity into ever deeper economic trouble and drawing the entire planet toward environmental catastrophe.

The view that human beings – through their growing numbers and their escalating levels of personal consumption – are inexorably outstripping the globe's capacity to sustain them is one of the most vivid, powerful, and enduring economic myths of the modern era. Since 1798, when T.R. Malthus wrote his famous *Essay on the Principle of Population*, the argument that the exponential growth of people and their demands will eventually result in what we would now call "overshoot" of "carrying capacity" – and in consequent catastrophe – has convinced successive generations of concerned scientists and most reporters that a serious "population problem" is imminent and requires urgent and immediate action.

The durability and influence of this notion is easy to understand, for the proposition is inherently plausible, and at first glance looks intuitively obvious.

The planet, after all, is of a fixed size. At some point a finite sphere will necessarily be unable to meet a geometrically rising demand upon its resources. Moreover, every other form of life on the planet is governed by the immutable and unforgiving biological laws that Malthus described: the regular tendency for a species to procreate beyond its environment's capacity to feed it, only to have its numbers brought back to "equilibrium" through brutal spikes in the death rate.

Yet a fundamental flaw lies at the heart of Malthusian economic reasoning: human beings are not like other animals. The Malthusian population-resource calculus does not consign our species to brutish subsistence. Our species, unlike all others, can consciously apply problem-solving techniques to the project of expanding its resource base and tempering its immediate environment.

Innovation Can Expand Humanity's Resource Base

Beasts cannot purposely transform their survival prospects. Human beings can – and they have done so dramatically across the entire planet. In 1900, the expectation of life at birth for the world as a whole was probably about 30 years. Today, according to projections by the United Nations Population Division, it is probably over 65 years – more than twice as high as a century ago.

In areas of the globe widely assumed to be most prone to Malthusian calamity, the improvements in longevity have been especially striking. During the past half-century, according to the UN's figures, life expectancy for the grouping of low-income countries known as the "less developed regions" has jumped by more than half – an increase of more than 23 years. During the same period, the overall infant mortality rate for the poorer countries is believed to have fallen by almost two-thirds. Humanity, in short, is in the midst of a "health explosion," and it is this health explosion – not some improvident shift in procreation patterns – that entirely accounts for the unprecedented "population explosion" of the 20th century.

These tremendous and sustained worldwide improvements in health for our species speak to another crucial distinction between human beings and all other animals: The same factors that have made our health revolution possible – advances in scientific and technological knowledge, the spread of education, improvements in organizational technique, and the like – have also supported a spectacular, and ongoing, increase in human productivity. Thanks to productivity improvements, human beings, unlike any other living creatures, can progressively and intentionally augment the "resource base" that sustains them.

The point is vividly illustrated by the race between population and food over the course of the 20th century. Traditional Malthusian doctrine maintains that food production cannot keep pace with mankind's ability to multiply (due to the geometric "power of population" and the "law of diminishing returns"). The 20th century tested that proposition: for the past 100 years, human numbers multiplied at a pace never before recorded. Between 1900 and 2000, the world's population is thought to have nearly quadrupled, surging from perhaps 1.6 or 1.7 billion to more than six billion.

But this extraordinary population explosion did not consign humanity to mounting hunger. Just the opposite: As the doubling of global life expectancy during the 20th century attests, mankind enjoys a far better diet today than when the Earth's population was only one-fourth as large. To be sure, millions upon millions of people on our planet still live under the threat of deadly hunger. Yet such tragic circumstances are now, finally, the distinct exception rather than the rule of the human condition.

Despite Growing Populations, Food Is Cheaper Than Ever

The inescapable fact is that never before has humanity been as well fed as it is today – and those improvements in our nutritional well-being have coincided with the most massive and rapid population increase in the human experience. Indeed, despite our species' exponentially increasing demand for food, there is compelling economic evidence that foodstuffs are actually growing ever less scarce.

Figure 5-1 illustrates this point, comparing the 20th century's global population trends with the inflation-adjusted international price trends for the three major cereal grains: corn, wheat, and rice. As may be seen, real prices for those three cereals have plummeted by more than 70 percent

Figure 5-1

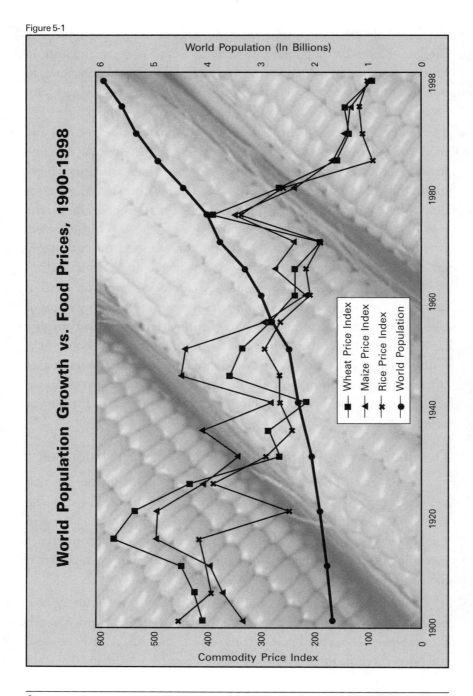

World Population Growth vs. Food Prices, 1900-1998

since 1900. Of course, these price declines were not smooth; the graph shows recurrent and sharp perturbations. Yet the century's sharp temporary upswings in prices are explained better by political disruptions – World War I, World War II, the Korean War, and the government-exacerbated "world food crisis" of the early 1970s – than by either demographic or environmental events.

The long-term fall in cereal prices bears directly on the assessment of the availability of food in the modern world. Prices are meant to measure scarcity. By the information that prices are meant to convey, foodstuffs would seem to be significantly less scarce at the end of the 20th century than they were at its beginning – even though mankind is now consuming far more of them today than in the past.

For other species, unchecked procreation will predictably exhaust available food supplies, but human ingenuity and action has resulted in an accumulation of innovations and cost-reducing arrangements that meet humanity's rapidly growing nutritional needs. Thus, global population has risen at an average pace of about 1.3 percent a year for a century, yet global cereal prices have simultaneously fallen at a tempo of nearly 1.3 percent per annum. Never have more people inhabited the world than today -- and never before has food been so abundantly available for each of our planet's inhabitants.

Prices for Other Commodities Have Tumbled as Well

Faced with incontestable data concerning the race between mouths and food, a sophisticated neo-Malthusian would retort that food is only one of many resources upon which people depend and, given its insatiable desire for improved consumption, mankind's appetite for resource use – which spirals upward even more rapidly than its population levels – must eventually come into disastrous collision against some limiting natural constraint.

It is impossible today to disprove predictions about tomorrow, but the record of the recent past does not comport with the neo-Malthusian's proposed tableau of a world being steadily denuded of resources by unchecked population growth and consumerism. Paradoxically, despite humanity's burgeoning and indeed accelerating demand for consumption, global natural-resource constraints over the past century have not obviously been tightening – and by some important indications even appear to have been loosening.

That paradox is underscored in Figure 5-2, which contrasts estimated aggregate real global GDP with relative prices for primary commodities over the 20th century. The GDP estimates, prepared by the eminent economic historian Angus Maddison, cover 56 countries that as of 1992 comprised almost 90 percent of the world's population and more than 90 percent of the world's output, and thus provide a reasonably close approximation of total global product. The Relative Primary Commodity Price index, developed by the economists Enzo R. Grilli and Maw Cheng Yang, takes the international cost of a market basket of 24 of the most commonly consumed "renewable and non-renewable resources" – foodstuffs, non-food agricultural goods, and metals – and deflates them by an index of prices for manufactured products. Maddison's estimates extend from 1900 to 1992; Grilli and Yang's from 1900 to 1986. Inevitable, highly technical questions notwithstanding, both series may be viewed as authoritative for the trends they depict.

Between 1900 and 1992, by Maddison's reckoning, global GDP grew at a rate of almost three percent a year, or more than twice the pace of population growth. Between 1900 and 1992, this made for an amazing fourteen-fold increase in the estimated planetary product. This means that the global population's demand for goods and services also soared by a factor of 14 during those years.

But despite this staggering increase in demand, the relative price of non-fuel primary commodities dropped – and dropped markedly. Between 1900 and 1986, the cumulative decline in the relative prices of these goods was about 40 percent; this long-term decline trended -0.6 percent a year.

One may object that this primary commodity index excludes fuels – natural resources that are patently non-renewable and also, arguably, increasingly scarce – and that the omission biases the trends depicted. But adding oil and coal to the primary commodity market basket changes

Figure 5-2

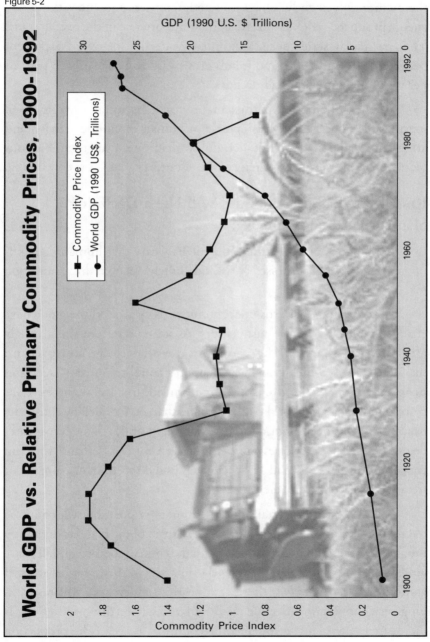

World GDP vs. Relative Primary Commodity Prices, 1900-1992

the picture only slightly. One Grilli and Yang series includes those two energy products, weighted to reflect their importance in the overall trade. That particular series posts a cumulative decline of over 35 percent between 1900 and 1986, and trends downward at a pace of -0.5 percent per year for eight and a half decades.

To the convinced Malthusian, it would be unfathomable, even inexplicable, that such a vast increase in human economic activity, and attendant material demands, would coincide with an unambiguous reduction in the measured scarcity of the resources people were consuming.

Knowledge-Based Economies Will Use a Declining Share of Earth's Resources

Looking toward the future, the media worry that human demands upon a fragile planet are poised to rise indefinitely. Yet even this assumption may be wrong.

For one thing, patterns of economic activity around the globe have changed radically over the past century. As societies become increasingly affluent, the share of the economy devoted to agriculture and manufacturing – which draw heavily upon natural resources – decreases progressively, while the share accounted for by services rises correspondingly. The World Bank estimates that services already constitute over three-fifths of the world's total economic output. To an ever-greater degree, modern economies are being driven by the demand for, and consumption of, skills and knowledge embodied in human beings, not treasures extracted from the earth.

It is also far from certain that the human population will continue to grow in the coming millennium, even with all of the benefits of orderly progress. In every industrialized society in the contemporary world, fertility levels are below the replacement level – in some of them, far below it. If continued, *ceteris paribus*, these childbearing preferences will result in long-term population decline. Sub-replacement fertility, moreover, is increasingly prevalent in low-income countries as well. The proportion

CHAPTER 5

♦

THE MEDIA'S MYTH:
Too Many People, Too Few Natural Resources

"Ultimately, no problem may be more threatening to the Earth's environment than the proliferation of the human species." – Anastasia Toufexis, "Overpopulation: Too Many Mouths," article in *Time*'s special Planet of the Year edition, January 2, 1989.

"A newborn baby, hardly most people's idea of a poster child for a worldwide problem, but with the United Nations saying person number 6,000,000,000 is being born somewhere on Earth about now, some say a growing population is the greatest problem facing humanity." – Natalie Pawelski, CNN's *TalkBack Live*, October 12, 1999.

"More people also means more cities – half the world is expected to live in urban areas within five years. And more pavement means less open land, less space for the other creatures on our planet, though India has actually started to slow its rate of growth, bringing fertility rates down." – Lynn Sherr, *ABC 2000* News Special, December 31, 1999.

"Relentless human expansion is the main reason the world is fast losing its biodiversity, raising the specter that we will eventually live, in the words of writer David Quammen, on a 'planet of weeds.' If that danger doesn't seem imminent, consider this: sprawl is paving over the land we need to grow our food." – Dick Thompson, "Asphalt Jungle," article in *Time*'s special Earth Day 2000 edition, April-May 2000.

"The U.S. foreign aid program was born out of the Marshall Plan, which helped rebuild Europe after World War II. We learned from the mistakes we made after World War I, when a devastated Europe was left to fester. Misery, poverty, hopelessness, overpopulation and environmental degradation breed wars. We see that in the civil wars raging around the globe: too many people for too few resources." – Judy Mann, "Proclaiming the Wonders of Family Planning," *Washington Post* column, July 14, 2000.

of humanity living in countries with sub-replacement fertility is rapidly approaching the 50 percent mark, and for the rest of the world fertility is falling steadily.

Reliable long-term population projections are impossible, owing to the fact that future birth rates are unknowable today. One may note, however, that if the pace of global fertility decline observed over the past thirty-five years were to continue for another quarter century, human numbers would peak around the year 2040, and thereafter the population would begin to decline.

None of this is to suggest that concern with humanity's current and prospective impact on the global environment is unwarranted. Quite the contrary. Strident and confident assertions by Malthusians and eco-activists notwithstanding, we understand all too little today about this extraordinarily complex dynamic. Under any circumstances, the case for conservation of, and stewardship over, natural resources would seem compelling. Yet responsible conservation and stewardship cannot be promoted by a worldview that strips mankind of its unique dignity, any more than the Earth's "carrying capacity" for human beings can be established through rules and parameters derived from populations of fruit flies.

CHAPTER 6

◆

MEDIA MYTH:

The United States Should Be More Like Europe

William A. Niskanen

At various times, critics of the American economy have suggested that we ought to be more like Japan or Europe. The news media regularly trumpet Europe as a continent with superb health care, child care, job security, job training, and public safety – especially compared with the United States. Europe's "third way" economies are often portrayed as more compassionate and efficient than the more market-oriented U.S. economic system.

It has not always been the Western European model that the media have showcased and admired. Years ago, many in the American media praised the Soviet model. Fortunately, Eastern European statism did not survive the Soviet Union's collapse and no longer has many advocates outside the sheltered groves of academe. Many journalists credited the Japanese model of industrial policy for the relatively high rate of Japanese economic growth through the 1980s, and the Japanese model thus became attractive to many business groups that were seeking similar subsidies and protection from competition. Sluggish economic growth in Japan during the 1990s does not seem to have embarrassed the advocates of the Japanese model – but it has substantially reduced their audience.

The latest rage is the European "social market" model, under which employers, labor unions, and the government work out agreements to reduce potential class conflicts. But the appeal of this model is now threatened by sustained high unemployment rates that are far above U.S. levels.

CHAPTER 6

♦

Although conditions differ somewhat among the European countries, the most important common characteristics of the European labor market are a centralized wage-setting process, governmental restrictions on firing, and relatively generous unemployment benefits of extended duration. The media typically boast about these generous benefits without noting the costs. It turns out the costs are substantial.

Higher Pay for Lower-Rung Workers, but Fewer Jobs

One consequence of these high benefits is a compression of wages at the bottom of the wage distribution, increasing the lowest wage relative to the median wage. While this increases the earnings of the employed, it also reduces the incentive of workers to improve their skills and reduces the incentive of employers to hire the least skilled. At the same time, the restrictions on a private company's ability to fire an employee reduces its incentives to hire new workers, transforming labor from a variable input into a capital input. The generous unemployment compensation that is common in European countries also reduces the incentive of the unemployed to quickly find new work.

The combination of these characteristics has led to low employment growth, high unemployment rates, unusually high long-term unemployment rates, and high government expenditures for unemployment and welfare. Table 6-1 and Figure 6-1 summarize these conditions for the major European countries and the United States.

Since 1995, employment conditions in Europe and the United States have sharply diverged. In August 1999, the standardized unemployment rate in OECD Europe was 9.2 percent, while the U.S. rate had fallen to 4.2 percent. European labor policies have reduced the variance of wages in the bottom half of the wage distribution, but only at a great cost in other employment conditions. The labor market arrangements that led to this combination of wage and employment conditions in Europe are not the best model for the United States.

Sustained high unemployment, the pressures of globalization, and some country-specific conditions have led to different responses among

---

MEDIA MYTH: THE UNITED STATES SHOULD BE MORE LIKE EUROPE

Table 6-1

The U.S. Has a Higher Employment Rate and Higher Employment Growth

Percent	Civilian Employment	
	Rate 1995	Change 1985-95
France	48.8	+3.3
Germany	49.7	+6.5
Italy	41.8	-2.4
Spain	44.2	+9.4
U.K	56.7	+6.2
U.S.	62.9	+16.5

German rates are only for the former West Germany.
Spanish rates are for 1994 and 1984-94.

the European countries. Contrary to all economic logic, French Prime Minister Lionel Jospin seems insistent on reducing the work week in his country from 39 hours to 35, and he has proposed raiding the social insurance fund to compensate employers for the lost output. This proposal provoked a massive strike in early 2000 by French truck drivers, who fear that they will lose jobs to haulers outside France. And the French employers' association recently voted to resign their role in an arrangement among employers, labor unions, and the government that has managed pensions, unemployment insurance, and other elements of the French safety net.

The German government borrowed heavily in the 1990s to finance the reunification, leaving a smaller budget for other government programs. German industry found itself burdened with both high taxes and high labor costs, leading some German firms to establish new plants in other countries. The labor unions, fearing a loss of jobs, have pressured the government for continued job security. Germany has also been rocked by a major political scandal, in which former French President Francois Mitterand was alleged to have arranged a $16 million bribe to the German

Christian Democratic Party in a deal with then-German Chancellor Helmut Kohl for a French firm to acquire an oil refinery in the former East Germany. The "social market" model seems to be breaking up on its home ground.

In the United States, the transition from school to work has little structure and is not very effective, but there is little agreement on what might work better. Training systems based on the German model might seem to be an attractive alternative. In the countries that use this system,

Figure 6-1

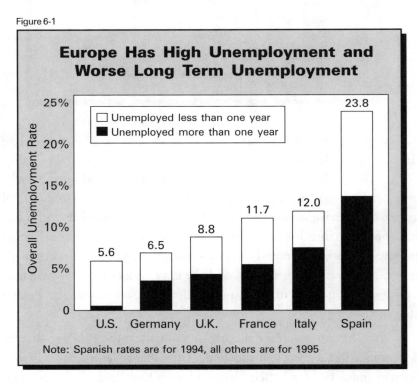

a majority of those age 16 through 19 spend most of the work week in worksite training, augmented by one or two days of related school studies. In Germany, more than 20 percent of employers participate in this system and about 60 percent of young people choose their vocation and their first job based on these apprenticeships.

THE MEDIA'S MYTH:
The U.S. Should Be More Like Europe

"The American health care system is high-tech and high-cost. We like to think it's the best in the world, and for some people it is. But...of the 16 democracies studied, the United States is the only one without government-guaranteed health insurance for everyone, and we're the country with the highest medical costs." – Hugh Downs, "Are We #1?" ABC's *20/20*, September 20, 1991.

"We're only kind of at the tip of the iceberg. We have a long way to go before we match up to European countries, don't we?" – ABC *Good Morning America* co-host Joan Lunden, talking about family leave with Ellen Galinsky of the Families and Work Institute, June 21, 1994.

"In Europe, though, workers call the American way 'cowboy capitalism.' Even with 12 percent unemployment in France, workers still get six-week vacations, unlimited sick days and free visits to spas in Germany. To keep all that, workers are striking. After all, our bright economic statistics do carry a heavy price." – Ray Brady, *CBS Evening News*, August 25, 1997.

"It's called the American work ethic, and some say it could be killing us.... Europe has the idea. Ever wonder why almost every American tourist spot is filled with foreign tourists? One reason: Europeans have two weeks more vacation than Americans." – Jim Avila, *NBC Nightly News*, June 12, 2000.

"How does this sound to you: shorter working hours, longer holidays and no paycuts? Economists said, 'No way Jose, or Josette,' but the French are making it work. Unemployment is down, the French economy is strong and workers are smiling a lot more these days....The French, they've got it right, don't they?" – Katie Couric, NBC's *Today*, August 1, 2001.

American educators and employers, however, reject the German model, reflecting a concern about early tracking and narrow vocational specialties that are characteristic of this system. In this case, the German model seems to work well for some European countries, but it does not appear to be the right model for school-to-work transition in the United States.

Europe Is Not Like the United States

Europe is now embarked on a new experiment based on an American model – a common currency for most of the countries in the European Union. The conditions that have made a common currency work well in the United States, however, do not exist in Europe. In the United States, there is substantial mobility of labor among employers, industries, and the states; in Europe, there is much less labor mobility, even within the same country. In the United States, the federal government provides substantial fiscal assistance to states experiencing temporary economic problems; the smaller European Union grants do not vary much with the current economic conditions of the EU countries.

Some time ago, I made the case that adoption of the Euro would have the following effects among the participating countries:

- The variance of the unemployment rates among the participating countries would increase.

- The political demands for changing the EU regional subsidies would increase.

- The Euro would prove to be a weaker currency than the German mark.

- One or more European governments would withdraw from the European Monetary Union following the first or second major differential economic shock.

The first three of these expectations have already been realized. Ireland and Spain are booming, while economic growth in the larger member countries is sluggish. This has led to pressures to reduce the EU subsidies to the more rapidly growing countries. And the Euro has declined some 20 percent relative to the dollar since its introduction in January 1999. Europe has not yet experienced a major differential shock since the introduction of the Euro, so the last expectation has yet to be tested.

The common lesson from the record of the German model of vocational training and the American model of a common currency is that they are not necessarily the best model for other countries or regions, even though they may be considered unusually successful in their home countries. Conditions may differ enough among countries that a policy model that works well elsewhere would not be a successful model in another country. At the same time, it is important to compare the experiences among different policy regimes as part of the process of evaluating the combination of policies in one's own country.

The most important lesson that I draw from the experience of the European "social market" model is that it is not the best model for the United States, whether or not it survives the problems that it now faces in Europe.

CHAPTER 7

♦

MEDIA MYTH:

The Shrinking Middle Class

W. Michael Cox

The image of the United States regularly portrayed by the media is one of class division. While most of us take middle-class life for granted, a few analysts see this American icon as an endangered species. Our hyperkinetic modern economy, they worry, exerts a centrifugal force of sorts, spinning households toward the top and bottom rungs of the income distribution and hollowing out the great middle of society. We also hear it said that the middle class is worse off today – working harder for less pay – than was the case 25 years ago.

The notion of a declining middle class amounts to an attack on the American economic model, i.e., if capitalism can't maintain the lifestyle of the great mass in the middle, then it has failed, creating an excuse for government intervention to make things right.

But the skeptics are wrong. We are largely a middle class nation, with rising levels of affluence. We are quite comfortable with our myriad creature comforts. Like most economic myths, that of the decline of the middle class comes from a misreading of some data and a failure to give full weight to signs of giant economic gains for American workers over recent decades.

The Middle Class Is Alive and Well

When we look at what's really going on in U.S. households, there's no doubt that more Americans than ever are enjoying a wealthier

---

♦

---

lifestyle. Indeed, the typical family has never had it better, thanks to a record-shattering economic expansion and a technology revolution that is delivering all kinds of new goods and services.

Pessimists who sound the alarm about a vanishing middle class find their smoking gun in data on the distribution of income among American households. According to the Census Bureau, the percentage of American families earning between one-half and two times the median income fell from 67.2 percent in 1969 to 61.2 percent in 1996.

Such a small statistical erosion should not normally be cause for alarm. But the popular press treated it as such, even though this allegedly bad news is really good news. For one thing, families graduating from the middle class into the richer category outpaced those slipping backward into poverty by a factor of three to one. The middle class is shrinking only to the extent that the middle class is growing richer.

The bigger distortion lies in measuring well-being by household income. When it comes to comparisons over time, these measures become tricky. With each passing generation, families have gotten smaller and more diverse. Even the straightforward dollars-and-cents of "income" doesn't stay the same over time; workers now receive more of their compensation in the form of non-cash fringe benefits.

Consumption offers a direct measure of living standards. The touchstones of our middle-class lifestyle are fairly obvious – home ownership, a car, household appliances, a secure nest egg, recreational opportunities, education for our children. The list could go on and on, with each family having its own version of the American Dream, but these goods and services define what it really means to be middle class in America.

Today's Working Americans Live Better than Yesterday's Millionaires

If the middle class were eroding, it would surely show up in what we consume. It doesn't. By every measure, as Table 7-1 illustrates, more American households have access to the goods and services typically associated with rising affluence. If anything, the standards for what is

Table 7-1

The Middle Class: Better Off in Every Way

Item	1970	Latest
Average size of a new home (square feet):	1,500	2,190
Homes with a telephone:	87%	94%
New homes with central heat & air conditioning:	34%	83%
New homes with a garage:	58%	86%
Households with one or more vehicles:	79.6%	92.1%
Households with two or more vehicles:	26.8%	60.4%
Households with a color TV:	34.0%	97.9%
Households with cable TV:	6.3%	66.1%
Households with clothes washer:	62.1%	83.2%
Households with clothes dryer:	44.6%	75.0%
Households with frost-free refrigerator:	<25%	86.8%
Households with dishwasher:	26.5%	54.6%
Households with a microwave oven:	<1%	90%
Households with a VCR:	0%	91%
Households with answering machine:	0%	71%
Households with cordless phone:	0%	73%
Households with cellular phone:	0%	68%
Households with camcorder:	0%	32%
Households with CD player:	0%	54%
Households with computer:	0%	53%
Per capita consumption of bottled water:	<1	13.1
Air miles traveled per capita:	646	2,259
Median household net worth (1999 dollars):	$28,373	$71,600
Mean household net worth (1999 dollars):	$87,436	$282,500
Life expectancy at birth (years):	70.8	76.5
Death rate, all causes (age-adjusted, per 100,000):	714.3	478.2
Injury rate (per 100):	29.6	21.7
Average work week:	37.1 hours	34.5 hours
Annual paid vacations and holidays:	15.5 days	22.5 days
Number of people retired from work:	13.3 million	27.5 mil.
Household daily hours:minutes spent watching TV:	5:59	7:12
Annual movies attended per person:	4.5	5.2
Annual hours spent viewing videos at home:	0	49
Adult softball teams:	29,000	178,000
Recreational golfers:	11.2 million	26.5 mil.
Amusement parks:	362	1,164
Attendance at pro sporting events (per 100,000):	24,766	44,180

middle class have risen with each past generation, with what were once luxuries for the rich becoming everyday items for the masses.

Start with the home. Two-thirds of Americans, a record, now own their own homes. Compared with 1970, today's new houses are larger and far more likely to have air conditioning and garages. The vast majority of U.S. households possess color televisions, washers, clothes dryers, and frost-free refrigerators. Nearly two-thirds of U.S. households have two or more cars.

In today's America households have products that no middle-class family could even imagine owning a generation ago. Videocassette recorders, answering machines, cellular telephones, compact disc players, and personal computers all burst onto the marketplace within the past two decades. Now, each of these gadgets is found in more than half of U.S. homes. One in three families owns a camcorder.

The modern marketplace delivers more variety, too, providing consumers a choice of 1,212 styles of vehicles, 790 magazine titles, 340 breakfast cereals, 185 television channels, 141 over-the-counter pain relievers, and 87 soft-drink brands. Some may dismiss the multiplicity of products as wasteful. It isn't. We are better off when we are able to buy products that offer exactly the right color, taste, style, or fit.

In many other ways, day-to-day life for the typical American family keeps getting better. Households' median net worth has more than doubled since the early 1970s. Vacation hours are longer, work hours are shorter. Death and injury rates are going down, we're living longer. America boasts more high school and college graduates. We've seen a democratization of leisure pursuits - more golfers, more vacationers on cruises, more outings to amusement parks, sporting events and cultural activities.

Middle class life improved during the 20th century. A good rule of thumb: Goods and services begin to enter the domain of the middle class when they reach 20 percent of the population. They become solidly middle class as their penetration moves past 50 percent.

The telephone first became a middle-class product in 1907, but it didn't reach half the country until after World War II. Electricity,

CHAPTER 7

◆

THE MEDIA'S MYTH:
The Shrinking Middle Class

"Most Americans view themselves as middle class. They define their lives by the jobs they have and the homes they live in. But the middle class is shrinking, and the expectation that our children will be able to live in homes like these, and have lives that are better than our own, is withering." – Harry Smith, *CBS Reports: Who's Getting Rich? And Why Aren't You?* August 8, 1996.

"Changes in the economy in recent decades have narrowed the middle class, led to stagnant wage and productivity growth and fundamentally altered the nature of jobs and work relationships.... Profits are being funneled to shareholders while workers' wage growth is stunted. Technological advances are replacing well-paying manufacturing jobs. The result, some predict, will be a two-tiered society..." – Jill Hodges, "How can more of us prosper in a more competitive economy?" *Minneapolis Star Tribune*, September 29, 1996.

"As these Californians in the middle look at the instant millionaires the New Economy is creating, many seem to fear that more and more Californians – including themselves and their families – are being economically left behind. Those middle-class fears are not baseless....The resurgent economic tide of the late '90s, driven largely by technology breakthroughs, did not raise the boats of those at and below the middle." – Mark Baldassare, "They See Dark Clouds on the Horizon in Our Sunny State," *Sacramento Bee*, January 2, 2000.

"Despite the remarkable advances, not everyone has been a beneficiary of the economic expansion, which is expected to break the record set between 1961 and 1969. Hundreds of thousands of workers – white- and blue-collar – lost jobs, wages for workers have not increased at the same rate as corporate profits or compensation for top management, and the gap between rich and poor has widened." – Kristine Henry and Bill Atkinson, "The Longest Boom," *Baltimore Sun*, January 30, 2000.

automobiles, radios, refrigerators, stoves, and clothes washers all spread into the middle class between the two world wars. In time, these goods became virtual entitlements for the middle class, reaching 75 percent of U.S. households and beyond.

Then came clothes dryers, dishwashers, air conditioning, and color television. In the past two decades, microwave ovens, cellular telephones, computers, and the Internet have filtered into the middle class. Indeed, new products are making their way into the middle class faster than ever before. It took hard-wired telephones three decades to reach half the nation. The cellular telephone took just three years to jump from 20 percent to 50 percent of U.S. households.

Realizing the American Dream Has Never Been Easier

What's behind the rising quality of middle class life? A long-term surge in productivity increased wages while reducing the cost of producing many goods and services. In terms of the currency that really matters – the work time it takes to buy products – just about everything we buy costs less than it did in past generations.

Based on the average manufacturing wage, the work-time "price" since 1970 fell 90 percent for color televisions, 71 percent for clothes washers, 51 percent for refrigerators, 96 percent for microwave ovens, 96 percent for coast-to-coast telephone calls, 25 percent for movie tickets and 18 percent for a McDonald's hamburger. Since their introduction, costs have plunged 99 percent for videocassette recorders, and 99 percent for cellular phones. (See Figure 7-1.) IBM's 8 megahertz PC-XT sold for $4,995 in 1983 – the equivalent of 566 hours of work excluding the monitor and other peripherals. Today's 466 megahertz models – including a monitor, color printer, fax modem and software – cost just 36 hours.

And the basics? A basket of 12 food staples, including bread, milk, coffee, and chicken, now goes for 30 percent less in terms of time on the job.

Getting more for less: That's how the middle class keeps expanding, and it is capitalism's promise, stated best by economist Joseph Schumpeter in *Capitalism, Socialism and Democracy:*

CHAPTER 7

◆

> The capitalist engine is first and last an engine of mass production, which unavoidably means also production for the masses....The capitalist process, not by coincidence, but by virtue of its mechanism, progressively raises the standard of life of the masses.... One problem after another of the supply of commodities to the masses has been successfully solved by being brought within the reach of the methods of capitalist production.

No ironclad standard for "middle class" exists. The concept, if it means anything at all, captures a living standard common to the broad center of society. The middle class cannot be worse off economically in a society where the vast majority of families are consuming more than ever before.

Figure 7-1

Decline in Work-Time Cost of Various Products
(Since 1970, Unless Otherwise Indicated)

Product	Change	Percent
Electricity	Down	11.3%
Refrigerators	Down	50.7%
Dryers	Down	59.6%
Washers	Down	70.9%
Color Televisions	Down	89.9%
Telephone Calls	Down	96.0%
Microwave Ovens	Down	96.4%
VCRs (since 1972)	Down	98.8%
Cell Phones (since 1984)	Down	99.1%
Home Computers (since 1984)	Down	99.9%

Free Markets Have Improved Middle Class Life

Even during times of prosperity, naysayers must not go unchallenged when they trash the free enterprise system. Refuting the notion of a declining middle class isn't just a matter of reviewing the statistics that reflect our economy. The intellectual battle over the fate of the middle class is another skirmish in a larger ideological war between capitalism's friends and foes.

CHAPTER 7

◆

There is no match for the free market's ability to deliver one of mankind's most important gifts – material progress. Even a millionaire in 1900 could not have made a long distance phone call, watched television, taken penicillin, brushed with fluoride toothpaste, flown on an airplane, enjoyed a blockbuster motion picture, escaped from the heat into air conditioning, received an organ transplant, or even taken an aspirin. None of these products was available in 1900; today, they are commonplace in just about every American community.

In short, it doesn't take $50 million or even $50,000 to live better, in many ways, than yesterday's millionaires. In the space of only three generations, the "masses" in America can afford what another era's robber barons could not have had at any price.

The middle class isn't shrinking. It's prospering as never before.

CHAPTER 8

◆

MEDIA MYTH:

Deregulation Hurts Consumers

Robert W. Crandall

The recent controversy swirling not over but in California regarding the deregulating of electric power has cast a cloud over economic deregulation generally. But before the entire notion of deregulation is discarded, it is important to note that California failed miserably because while it deregulated wholesale power, the state maintained its price controls on retail utilities, which were required to purchase power in the spot market during a period of sharply rising demand for energy.

In any case, what is undeniably true – but not widely reported by the media – is that deregulation has worked remarkably well in a variety of other sectors. In the last 20 years, the United States has successfully deregulated airline travel, trucking, railroads (partially), air cargo, long distance telephone service, telephone consumer equipment, natural gas extraction, banking services, and even oil production. In addition, attention is now being focused on opening electrical utility services and local telephone service to competition, if not deregulation.

Despite the enormous gains conferred upon consumers from these deregulatory exercises, it is surprising how often one reads in the press that deregulation has harmed consumers, either because it has allowed firms to increase prices, diminished service quality or, in the case of transportation deregulation, reduced public safety. The implicit premise involved in the observation that consumer prices will rise is that regulation constrains prices to levels lower than those produced in unfettered markets.

But such a result could only occur if these markets were not subject to competition, for any regulatory attempt to keep prices below competitive market levels would simply bankrupt some or all of the regulated firms.

The irony in all of this is that regulation generally inhibits competition, thereby allowing some prices to be raised above their competitive levels so as to provide the regulated firms with excess profits to subsidize other services targeted by the politically responsive regulators.

The two best case studies that expose the media myth that consumers have been hurt by deregulation are provided by airline travel and long distance telephone service. Both have been deregulated at the federal level, meaning that the market has been opened to entrants and prices are free to vary without government intervention.

Airline Deregulation: Lower Prices, Better Safety, and More Choices

The Airline Deregulation Act of 1978 ended airline regulation by phasing out the Civil Aeronautics Board (CAB) over a period of six years. Even before 1984, carriers were free to enter any domestic market and set their own fares. This created an early wave of new entrants – New York Air, Peoples Express, etc. – and a major realignment of the existing carriers' route structures. Many of the new entrants went bankrupt or were acquired, but the effect of entry and the expansion of Southwest Airlines was dramatic. Fares have declined dramatically since the early 1980s. (See Figure 8-1.) Equally important, the number of choices has expanded dramatically for all travelers.

Prior to deregulation, all carriers had to obtain approval from the CAB to serve any given route. The practical result of this rule was that no carrier was able to develop an efficient route structure. When deregulation arrived, carriers began to develop hub-and-spoke route structures that funnelled traffic to their major hubs for connecting flights throughout the country. As a result, travelers in smaller cities now have the option of taking a smaller plane to one of several nearby hubs and connecting to thousands of different flights around the world.

Figure 8-1

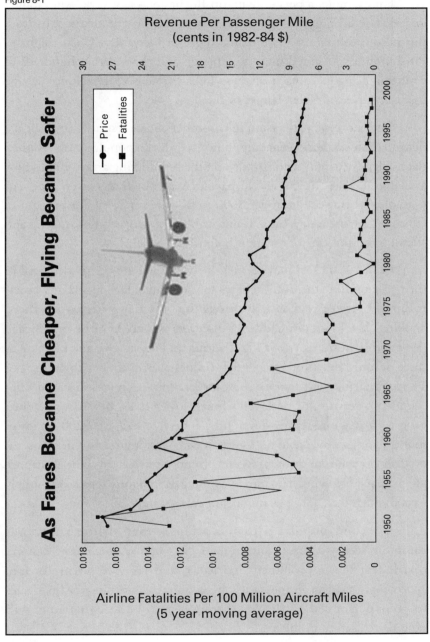

As Fares Became Cheaper, Flying Became Safer

Revenue Per Passenger Mile
(cents in 1982-84 $)

Airline Fatalities Per 100 Million Aircraft Miles
(5 year moving average)

For example, a person living in Rochester, New York, is no longer hostage to USAir for through flights to his or her final destination. Instead, this person can take a Continental flight to Newark, a USAir flight to Pittsburgh, or a United flight to Chicago and choose from hundreds of connecting flights in each of these hubs. Moreover, this choice can be made at various different times of the day.

The enormous expansion in consumer choice resulting from airline deregulation has gone generally unnoticed in the popular press. Rather, the media discussion tends to turn on the bewildering array of fares now available and the "ridiculous" disparities that exist at any given time. For example, it may cost a traveler $600 to fly one-way from Washington to Chicago O'Hare today, but a round-trip ticket between Los Angeles and Washington for a trip next month cost only $299.

At first glance, it may seem as if the airlines are being mercurial in their pricing. But the $600 reflects the "option value" for having access to hourly service to Chicago throughout the day with no advanced booking. If a journalist suddenly discovers she needs to be in Chicago this afternoon, she can get a flight within an hour or two and be there in three or four hours. It costs United Airlines a lot of money to have 14 or 15 jets available with empty seats for last-minute travel. It could offer round-trip service at Southwest's much lower rates, but it would then have to manage its space differently. Indeed, there are $200 or lower round-trip fares available on United from Washington to Chicago, but only on weekends or through special promotions with substantial advance purchase requirements. The traveler wishing to minimize travel costs simply sorts through the enormous number of choices and plans ahead.

A second popular misconception is that airline safety was compromised by deregulation. In their 1983 book *Dismantling America*, Martin Tolchin, a prominent journalist, and his wife Susan Tolchin, approvingly cited an airline critic's prediction that "opening the floodgates to inexperienced airlines through rapid deregulation will exacerbate...safety problems."

The ValuJet crash of a few years ago occurred on just such an airline, but this crash had nothing to do with the maintenance of the aircraft or the training of the pilots. More importantly, it has not been followed by other crashes on new airlines; as Figure 8-1 shows, airline safety has improved continually since deregulation.

As our incomes and wealth increase, we are willing to pay more and more for product safety, and sellers who do not offer such safety cannot survive in the marketplace where our preferences are registered. Even though the airline's planes and flight crews were not implicated in the ValuJet tragedy, the airline could not survive with its old name. When major carriers have had accidents, passengers have responded by avoiding them for a while, severely depressing their stock prices. As a result, their managements have every incentive to pursue safety – and they do.

It is worth noting that in 1998, when there was not a single commercial airline crash all year, the news received scarce attention, but a crash the next year made front-page headlines for many days – and deregulation was often cited as a problem.

The most serious criticism that consumers can levy against airline deregulation is that it has worked! Planes are much fuller because fares are lower and airlines have discovered how to manage their fare structures to assure maximum utilization of their aircraft. Car travel has also become safer since 1978, but it is still riskier than airline travel was in 1978 and much riskier than airline travel today.

Telephone Deregulation: Cheaper Long Distance and an End to Subsidized Local Service

Nowhere is there more nonsense offered about the effects of deregulation than in telecommunications. On a daily basis, we hear about the confusing bills and the rising cost of telephone service whose root cause is, allegedly, deregulation. In fact, such assertions are wrong on two counts: The telephone industry has not been fully deregulated, and the price of telephone service has fallen steadily for years (though not as rapidly as it might have fallen under full deregulation).

The telephone sector, like most others, was initially regulated at the industry's behest, but such regulation did not amount to much until after World War II. Since then, federal and state regulators have combined in response to populist pressures to keep local rates below cost for most residences outside major cities and even for some within city limits. The Faustian bargain was that long distance rates and certain business rates be kept far above cost to pay for underpriced local connections. The Federal Communications Commission (FCC) had to keep entrants out of long distance to maintain these cross subsidies, but it failed to keep MCI from breaking down the doors 25 years ago. Since that time, entry has pushed interstate long distance rates down steadily.

To its credit, the FCC eventually realized that keeping long distance rates artificially high in order to keep the flat local monthly rate low was sheer folly, since it discouraged the use of a valuable customer service. As a result, it has slowly raised the "federally mandated subscriber line charge" that appears on your local monthly bill so as to reduce the per-minute charges that local phone companies – the Bells and other small companies – assess the long distance companies for completing their calls. For their part, the states have been much slower to move in this direction. As a result, regulated intrastate long distance calls are often more expensive than longer, interstate calls.

The FCC finally deregulated interstate long distance service in 1995, although the Commission is still blocking entry of the local Bell companies into long distance service in response to the requirements of the 1996 Telecommunications Act. The market for "terminal equipment" – telephone receivers, modems, answering machines, fax machines, etc. – also was deregulated 20 years ago. In both markets, competition has replaced regulation in delivering the array of services and determining consumer prices. The long distance market is still dominated by a few large companies, but you may now buy the equipment you plug into your household telephone jacks from hundreds of different sellers.

Another "telephone service" – wireless cellular and PCS service – is completely deregulated. Neither the states nor the FCC attempt to control the price that you pay, nor the service quality you get, from your hand-held wireless phone. But even in this sector, competition was restrained by federal regulation until 1995, when the FCC began to auction the radio spectrum to competitive carriers in response to a congressional mandate. Prior to 1995, there were only two cellular providers in each market. Now there are five or six national carriers buying spectrum in FCC auctions and wiring the country. This has led to a staggering decline in rates charged consumers. (See Figure 8-2.)

Figure 8-2

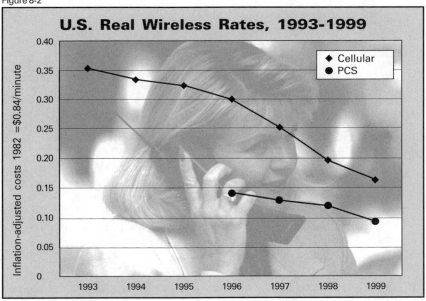

But have prices of telephone services risen recently, as critics of deregulation have argued? Hardly! The substitution of small monthly subscriber-line charges for long distance carrier access charges has been just one reason why long distance rates have fallen from 30 cents per minute or more a decade ago to just five cents per minute for the adroit shopper today. Each penny of reduction creates direct consumer benefits of $2 billion to $3 billion per year, not including the positive effects of lower telecommunications costs for business.

THE MEDIA'S MYTH:
Deregulation Hurts Consumers

"This is deregulation madness! We're going to have dirty water, dirty air. OSHA regulations are being rolled back. There's going to be no competition in the telecommunications industry, and between local cable and local phone, there's not going to be regulation at the present time. It's going to take a while and there's going to be no regulation in the meantime and so no, he [Clinton] can't go along with this, and the people, the public isn't going to go along with this. They don't want E. coli bacteria in their drinking water." – *Time* columnist Margaret Carlson, CNN's *Capital Gang*, August 5, 1995.

"No law passed by the last Congress caused politicians to heap more praise on themselves. The Telecommunications Act was supposed to be the greatest thing since Marconi: less regulation, more competition, lower rates...So where's all the competition? And what's happened to phone and cable bills?...Patience is now the big watchword of those who pushed this law through. It's a word that wasn't mentioned much when they were selling this plan a year ago." – Eric Engberg, *CBS Evening News*, March 5, 1997.

"We begin tonight with something to think about later this evening. You're at home or in the office or the car, and you go to make a phone call. What do you think the chances are that when you do you're going to be ripped off by the phone company? There are millions of complaints in this age of deregulation – millions – and it's a big enough issue for Congress to take up tomorrow." – Peter Jennings, ABC's *World News Tonight*, April 22, 1998.

"Why do airlines schedule more flights than airplanes can handle? It is a business decision, the airlines say, about gaining and keeping market share...To some degree, Congress started this problem. The deregulation of the airline industry made it cheaper to fly, but much more crowded." – Bob Woodruff, ABC's *World News Tonight*, July 21, 2000.

But the rate at which telephone rates are falling is far less than it should be. Not only is "deregulation" not raising prices, but continued regulation is clearly keeping them from falling as rapidly as they should. To see this, look at Figure 8-3, which compares the rate of change in long distance prices in the U.S. and Canada. The Canadians did not admit competition into long-distance services until 1992, at least 15 years after MCI forced its way into the U.S. market. Yet rates are already lower in Canada.

Figure 8-3

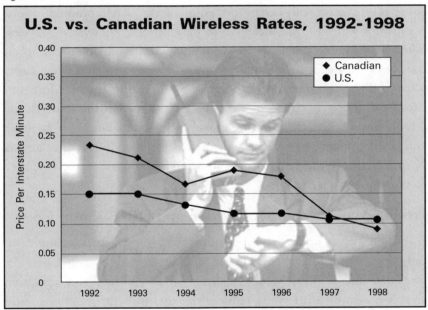

U.S. vs. Canadian Wireless Rates, 1992-1998

Have some people suffered from higher prices resulting from telephone "deregulation"? Sure, individuals who make very few long distance calls used to benefit from using the high price of those calls to subsidize their local bills. Those who make just one or two long distance calls may now have to pay their long distance carriers a few dollars each month for the privilege of having access to service and getting the bill. In a regulated environment, these people would probably be "protected" from such a charge by the excessive revenues received from the calls the rest of us make.

Regulation is always a political exercise to convey benefits on politically chosen constituencies at the expense of others. In the future, poor rural citizens – including the owners of ski condominiums in California, Utah, and Colorado – will probably have to pay the full cost of their lines if local service is ever truly deregulated. But don't panic – even if you live in the country, those wireless handsets will always be an option, and the cost of using them is falling like a stone.

The most important gains from telephone deregulation are still to come. If we ever get truly deregulated competition, all telecommunications companies will have the incentive to develop new, innovative services. Wireless and cable television companies are clearly moving ahead to do this, but regulated local companies must still wrestle with the regulators to offer their customers new services at remunerative prices. Moreover, because of a bizarre set of rules that have developed as the result of the 1996 Telecom Act, these local companies have to share their facilities with their competitors at regulated cost-based prices. Such requirements obviously reduce the gains from innovation and, therefore, the incentive to develop new services.

Freeing Markets Spurs Innovation and Drives Down Costs

The airline and telephone industries are only two examples of industries where full or partial deregulation has helped consumers. In every deregulated industry, the substitution of market forces for regulation creates pressure to innovate, reduces the cost of existing services, and drives prices toward costs. In most industries, consumer gains have been much greater than could have been predicted. The common media refrain that deregulation generally increases prices is simply incorrect even though prices to some consumers may rise – particularly if they had clout with regulators. Deregulation cannot benefit everyone, but the gains to the winners outweigh the cost to the losers.

CHAPTER 9

◆

MEDIA MYTH:

America Is Suffering from a Savings Crisis

William G. Gale

Journalists frequently contend that America is suffering from a savings crisis, and the government's official statistics on savings often seem to support the idea. But a closer look at how the numbers are put together and what they actually mean suggest that these fears are overblown.

Personal savings is one of the most closely watched but misunderstood economic indicators. For many years, the officially reported U.S. personal savings rate has been lower than that of many other industrialized countries. In recent years, the official measure of personal savings has plunged below zero at various times. During the first three quarters of 2000, the personal savings rate stood at just 0.1 percent of personal after-tax income. This is merely the continuation of a long downward trend in the rate, from 9.6 percent in the 1970s, to 9.1 percent in the 1980s, to 5.9 percent in the 1990s.

Some analysts think the low rate of personal savings signifies dangerously low levels of capital accumulation. For individuals, it raises fears that households are not putting enough money away for retirement or other purposes; for the economy as a whole, low savings could mean an increasing dependence on fickle foreign capital. But other observers think the decline in saving actually has been good news, since the accompanying rise in consumer spending has fueled the U.S. economic expansion and helped support the global economy – although some of these same analysts now worry that households are stretched too thin and will soon retrench, driving the U.S. and global economies into a tailspin.

Many experts, however, believe that standard measures of the savings rate in America are arbitrary and increasingly misleading. They concur with Yale economist William Nordhaus, who wrote, "Our tools for measuring saving and investment are stone-age definitions in the information age." In other words, we need to do a better job of defining and measuring what we mean by savings.

What Is Saving?

Saving is conventionally defined as income that is not consumed during a given period of time. By this measure, savings include funds that are stashed away in stocks, CDs, bank accounts, or retirement accounts, so the funds can be used for future consumption. A second definition of saving is the net change in wealth over time. Under this definition, if one's assets increase in value, then this increase in wealth, if it is not consumed, is a form of savings.

In theory, each of these definitions would provide the same measure of saving if "income," "consumption," and "wealth" were measured consistently. In practice, however, they are measured differently. Figure 9-1 compares trends in conventionally measured personal savings and trends in the change in net private-sector wealth. These two trends differ significantly, and the difference widened in the late 1990s, when capital gains were substantial.

Even if a particular definition of "saving" is accepted – for example, income minus consumption – the terms can be defined in different ways and saving measures can differ in scope. For example, a narrow measure of savings, often used in microeconomic studies of households, would concentrate on flows of financial assets and debt. On the other hand, a very broad measure of saving would focus on changes in the stock and value of financial, physical, intangible, human, public, natural, and environmental capital. Each variation of the scope of saving implies alternative measures of "income," "capital," "wealth," and so on.

Savings can be measured in either real or nominal terms, and either gross or net of depreciation (the decrease in value over time of plants,

Figure 9-1

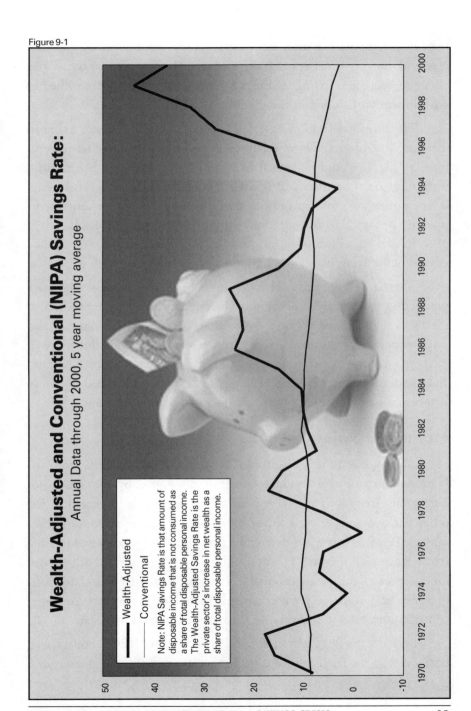

Wealth-Adjusted and Conventional (NIPA) Savings Rate:
Annual Data through 2000, 5 year moving average

— Wealth-Adjusted
— Conventional

Note: NIPA Savings Rate is that amount of disposable income that is not consumed as a share of total disposable personal income. The Wealth-Adjusted Savings Rate is the private sector's increase in net wealth as a share of total disposable personal income.

machines, equipment, homes, etc.). For most economic purposes, however, it is undoubtedly most appropriate to measure saving in real terms and net of depreciation. Saving measures can also vary with respect to whether government is included in the picture.

The proper definition of savings depends on what we are trying to measure. To understand how well households are preparing for retirement, for example, it would be logical to focus on personal wealth measures, including Social Security and Medicare benefits. In contrast, if the goal is to examine government policies that encourage saving for retirement, it would be logical to consider the effect on government saving as well as private saving, since policies that raise private saving but reduce government saving might not have the desired effect.

Alternatively, if the goal is to understand the share of aggregate production that society is devoting to investment in future production, it makes sense to include not only conventionally measured savings, but also investment in human capital, research and development, and other forms of intangible capital. It also makes sense to measure foreign capital flows into and out of the country. Whether capital gains should be included as savings is also an issue of some controversy, as discussed more fully below.

Measures of Saving

The figures quoted most often for personal saving come from the National Income and Product Accounts developed by the Bureau of Economic Analysis. The NIPA personal saving rate is measured as the difference between personal disposable income and personal consumption outlays. Personal income is derived by first calculating individual income from wages and salaries, other labor income, net income from unincorporated business, net rental income, personal interest and dividend income, and transfer payments. Subtracted from this are personal contributions for social insurance (Social Security and Medicare).

Several features are relevant for understanding the NIPA personal saving data. First, accrued and realized capital gains are excluded. A realized gain is the monetary gain from the sale of a stock or other asset. An accrued gain is the increase in the value of an asset that is not sold. Neither realized nor accrued capital gains are counted as savings in the NIPA framework.

Second, all contributions to, and interest and dividend earnings on, private pensions, 401(k)s, IRAs, and the pensions of government workers are included in personal saving.

Third, Social Security, which constitutes a huge proportion of the retirement wealth of most households, is treated differently than pensions. Social Security contributions are not counted in personal saving (they are subtracted as part of personal tax and non-tax payments), so Social Security benefits are counted as personal income (as transfer payments).

Fourth, NIPA treats consumer durables and owner-occupied housing differently, even though both are physical assets and both provide a stream of consumption benefits in the future. Spending on owner-occupied housing is considered saving, with the net imputed rental income included in the rental income component of personal income, and the imputed space rental in the services component of consumption expenditures. In contrast, purchases of other consumer durables count as current consumption outlays.

Fifth, the NIPA saving measure includes nominal interest receipts as income and nominal interest payments as outlays. In the presence of inflation, however, only the real component of interest flows should count as income or outlays. For example, if a corporation pays a household $100 in nominal interest, and the inflation rate and real interest rate are equal, real household-sector saving is overstated by $50 and real corporate saving is understated by $50.

Sixth, saving in the form of pensions has an implicit tax liability associated with it. For example, a household that makes a $100 tax-deductible contribution to a pension and is permanently in a 20 percent tax bracket should only be considered to have saved $80. The remaining $20 is deferred government taxes, representing neither current consumption nor increased future consumption for the household. Likewise, a similar proportion of interest and dividend earnings on pensions should not be construed as personal saving. NIPA personal saving measures, however, include the entire contribution and interest and dividend earnings on private pensions.

Corporate saving in the NIPA is the undistributed profit of corporations (i.e., after-tax profits less dividends paid to shareholders), plus an inventory valuation adjustment applied to the book value of inventories and a capital consumption adjustment applied to the book value of plant and equipment. Like personal saving, NIPA corporate saving does not adjust interest flows for inflation.

From the perspective of economic theory, the line between personal and corporate saving is thin and somewhat arbitrary. The distinctions that NIPA makes between personal and corporate saving do not appear to be the most relevant or appropriate for most economic models or analyses of saving. For example, corporate dividend payments and corporate share repurchases both involve shifting funds from the corporate to the household sector, but have different effects on sectoral saving in the NIPA.

A second measure of saving uses data on household balance sheets in the Federal Reserve Board's Flow of Funds Accounts (FFA) to examine how the composition of private and household saving has changed over time. The FFAs measure the value of wealth holdings and debt and the active acquisition and disposition of assets and liabilities. In recent years, the FFA and NIPA measures have moved in relatively similar ways.

What Do (Or Don't) the Saving Measures Tell Us?

Even this brief discussion of the saving measures shows that personal saving is a poor measure of how much the nation as a whole is saving. National saving has actually risen in recent years because corporate saving and government surpluses have increased more than personal saving has fallen.

Nor is personal saving even a good measure of how much households are saving. The official measure does not correct for inflation – it treats housing differently from other durable goods, and it does not adjust fully for taxes. The distinction between personal and corporate saving is also arbitrary and saving by non-profits is included as household saving.

These seeming technicalities make a big difference. For example, personal saving fell from 5.7 percent of GDP in the 1970s to less than zero in 1998 (under the definition of personal saving in use at that time). However, John Sabelhaus of the Congressional Budget Office and I found that a measure that conformed more closely to economic concepts of saving, by including businesses and households and adjusting for the other factors above, showed saving at nine percent of GDP in the 1970s and seven percent in 1998. These findings indicate that although saving has declined, the drop-off is much smaller, and the current level of saving is much higher than the official figures show.

The official figures also omit capital gains, which were six to ten times as large as official saving in the late 1990s, but which were hugely negative in 2000. If accrued gains are included, saving is at its highest level in at least 40 years, not its lowest. But should gains be included as saving? In some contexts, the answer is obvious. For an individual contemplating his retirement account, it makes perfect sense to include accruing capital gains as individual saving. Likewise, capital gains that reflect increases in a company's earnings should clearly be counted as saving. Current owners are enriched by the gain, but potential buyers are not made poorer; the cost of buying a claim on a dollar's worth of the company's profits has remained the same.

But some capital gains are not saving. Suppose the perceived riskiness of stocks – the so-called equity risk premium – falls. This would raise share prices, even if there were no increase in profits. Current shareholders would be wealthier, but potential buyers would be worse off because the cost of buying a dollar of future corporate profits would have gone up. In a closed economy, potential buyers are worse off by exactly as much as shareholders are better off, so there is no net wealth creation, or saving. In an open economy, the capital gain could represent national saving, but only to the extent that it increased Americans' ability to purchase goods from other countries.

In practice, there is a great, unresolved debate over why the stock market has risen to such previously unimagined heights. But if even a

THE MEDIA'S MYTH:
America Is Suffering from a Savings Crisis

"To make it in retirement, experts say people must save on their own. But the national savings rate of 3.9 percent is the lowest in 59 years. Two-thirds of all working Americans save little or nothing for retirement. It's a crisis, analysts say." – Mike Jensen, *NBC Nightly News*, June 4, 1998.

"Americans emptied their piggy banks and shopped relentlessly for cars and other big-ticket items in February, adding to the economic imbalance Federal Reserve Chairman Alan Greenspan is anxious to contain.... Economists fear that if the economy dips into recession, the low savings rate could exacerbate problems because many households would be left without cash to fall back on to help clear mounting debts carrying higher interest rates." – Mark Egan, "Americans' Buying Binge Shows Little Sign of Letting Up," *Los Angeles Times*, April 1, 2000.

"As a nation, America does not save enough. The problem has been reduced in recent years by the emergence of huge federal budget surpluses. Running surpluses allows the government to begin repaying the national debt, which is a form of savings. But the budget surpluses are unlikely to last more than 15 years, if that long, say budget analysts. And in the meantime the personal savings rate has dropped to almost nothing."– Richard Stevenson, "Troubles That Lurk Beneath Prosperity's Surface," *New York Times*, December 18, 2000.

"Japanese, German, Latin American investors have all put their savings in America rather than their own countries. Thank goodness, because we need the cash. These days, Americans spend more than they earn. So we depend on foreign investments and loans to make up the difference....If even a fraction of this money stopped coming into the United States, it could produce a spiral of problems: a falling dollar, which forces higher interest rates, which weakens stock prices and causes a sharper slowdown. It's a classic vicious cycle." – Fareed Zakaria, "Show Us the Money," *Newsweek*, March 26, 2001.

CHAPTER 9

♦

small portion — say 20 percent — of the market gains in the last decade represent increases in expected future profits, rather than changes in attitudes toward stocks generally, U.S. aggregate saving was high in the 1990s relative to its past performance.

In summary, the low officially reported savings rate for the U.S. is potentially problematic when it comes to our long-term economic growth potential. But a careful look behind the recent numbers shows that, under current conditions, there is no savings crisis.

This paper is based on "Perspectives on the Household Saving Rate,"
Brookings Papers on Economic Activity, 1999:1,
by John Sabelhaus and William G. Gale.

CHAPTER 10

◆

Why American Economists Can't Predict the Future

David Hale

One of the more striking features of the U.S. economy's outstanding performance from 1995-2000 was the unwillingness of most economists to believe it could happen. Yet these same experts, regardless of their track records, remain a key source for journalists, who routinely lard stories – on issues as diverse as tax cuts, future government surpluses, and welfare reform – with the pessimistic pronouncements of analysts who have failed to appreciate the strength and stamina of the U.S. economy.

On the first business day of every year, the *Wall Street Journal* publishes a survey of forecasts from Wall Street firms and major corporations about the economic outlook. On the basis of the *Journal* survey, the U.S. forecasting community has been consistently too bearish about the American economy's growth performance. During the period 1994-1999, the economists projected an average annual growth rate of only 2.3 percent for the U.S. economy, compared to an actual outcome of close to 3.9 percent.

That's a very large error for professionals whose jobs are to predict the future direction of the U.S. economy. Nor has their bias been random; their overwhelming skew has been toward undue pessimism:

- In 1994, the average forecast in the *Wall Street Journal* survey projected an annualized growth rate of 2.8 percent for both the first and second half of the year. The actual outcome was 3.6 percent output growth and a doubling of U.S. short-term interest rates to hold inflation in check.

- In 1995, forecasters compensated for their 1994 error by jacking up growth forecasts to annual rates of 2.9 percent for the first half of 1995 and 2.2 percent for the second half. As a result of the Mexico crisis, though, growth slowed sharply to only 2.3 percent for the year.

- In 1996, forecasters reverted to subdued growth forecasts and projected rates of only 1.8 percent output growth during the first half of 1996 and 2.0 percent during the second half. The actual result was 3.3 percent for the year.

- In 1997, forecasters continued to look for a slowing in the economy and were even more wrong than during 1996 because output grew at a 3.9 percent annual rate.

- In 1998, forecasters increased their growth projections modestly to annualized rates of 2.4 percent during the first half and 2.1 percent during the second half, but the economy again out-performed by expanding at a 3.6 percent annual rate.

- In 1999, forecasters began the year projecting only 1.9 percent output growth during the first half and 2.2 percent during the second half. The actual outcome was a growth rate twice as high as the consensus expected.

The cumulative forecasting error of professional economists for the period 1994-1999 was so large that the economy expanded at a rate *40 percent higher* than the consensus predicted for those years.

Predictions Turned Positive Despite Warning Signs

More recently, American forecasters belatedly caught up with the economy's growth momentum. In July of 1999, they raised their growth forecasts for that year to 4.0 percent and produced preliminary forecasts for 2000 calling for 2.6 percent output growth. Six months later, they boosted growth forecasts for 2000 to 4.6 percent and estimated that output growth during 2001 could remain as high as 3.0 percent. As of mid-July 2000, they were projecting 4.8 percent output growth for the year, compared to 3.3 percent for 2001. The economy's performance has been so benign for so long that forecasters have had little choice but to raise their output growth forecasts.

Yet, what is interesting about recent revisions is how unconcerned forecasters have become about several shocks still in progress. There has been a large rise in oil prices which has cost consumers about $75 billion, but forecasters did not expect it to have any lingering impact on either spending or inflation expectations. The Federal Reserve raised interest rates by 175 basis points from 1999-2000, but analysts in the summer of 2000 had not changed their view that incremental monetary policy changes would not prevent growth from remaining near a 3.0-3.5 percent trend line. The current account deficit will soon reach 5.0 percent of GDP, but the U.S. has had so much success in attracting capital inflows that most analysts assume the dollar will remain resilient indefinitely.

The complacency among economists today, and the widespread pessimism apparent two years ago, suggests several things about the U.S. forecasting community.

First, American forecasters are very much trend followers. During the mid- and late-1990s, it was commonly assumed that the economy's trend growth rate was about 2.0 to 2.5 percent, so most forecasts clustered in that range. Today, it is widely assumed that the trend growth rate could be as high as 3.0 or 3.5 percent, so most forecasts now hover in that range.

Secondly, the forecasting community was slow to grasp the impact of the information-technology revolution on productivity growth, stock market performance, and wealth creation in the economy. The boom in the IT sector boosted the economy's growth rate to 2.7 percent during the period 1992-1997 from a level which might otherwise have been only 2.2 percent. It also encouraged the market capitalization of the technology sector of the stock market to expand from $300 billion a decade ago to about $4.5 trillion recently. It triggered an IPO boom on the NASDAQ, which also has helped to fuel an expansion of venture capital funding to levels as high as $50 to $60 billion per annum from only $5 to $6 billion in the mid-1990s.

This venture capital activity guarantees that the U.S. will continue to enjoy a high level of new company formation and technological progress. What remains unclear, though, is whether the IT revolution will be able to support a high level of productivity growth even as monetary policy gradually reduces the rate of output growth. This issue will have a critical impact on the economy's performance because any faltering of productivity will boost unit labor costs and increase pressure on firms to raise prices. In such an environment, the Fed could feel compelled to raise interest rates further and risk driving the economy to a growth rate far below new perception of its optional trend.

Thirdly, economists often react to a shock by focusing only on its initial impact and not on its secondary consequences. A good example is the Asia crisis of 1998. Many economists slashed their 1998 growth estimates because they expected the Asia crisis to produce a large expansion of the U.S. trade deficit and depress manufacturing. They were correct about the initial effect of the Asia slump, but failed to understand three benign consequences of the crisis for the U.S. economy:

- It caused the Federal Reserve to put monetary policy on hold and delay interest rate changes despite the fact that the U.S. had achieved a full employment economy.

- It produced a large decline in global commodity prices (oil, copper, nickel, etc.), which lowered U.S. inflation at a time of rising wages and thus helped to boost consumer spending.

- It further enhanced the relative attractiveness of the U.S. equity market, encouraging a sharp rise in U.S. equity prices, and a decline in the household savings rate which reinforced the upward momentum in retail sales.

American economists misjudged the growth consequences of the Asia crisis because they focused on the trade account rather than the capital account.

Table 10-1

Blue Chip Economic Forecast				
	INFLATION		**UNEMPLOYMENT**	
YEAR	**Forecast**	**Actual**	**Forecast**	**Actual**
1994	2.8%	2.6%	6.3%	5.5%
1995	3.1%	2.8%	5.6%	5.6%
1996	2.7%	3.0%	5.8%	5.4%
1997	2.9%	2.3%	5.4%	4.7%
1998	2.2%	1.6%	4.8%	4.4%
1999	2.0%	2.2%	4.7%	4.1%
2000	2.7%	2.5%	5.3%	3.9%
Average				
1994-00	2.6%	2.4%	5.4%	4.8%

Wrong Predictions May Lead to Wrong Policies

The forecasting errors of economists can have real negative effects on the economy and can even become self-fulfilling prophecies. Faulty forecasts can cause bad policy decisions. The Federal Reserve did not raise interest rates during a major boom in both the economy and the stock market during 1998-1999 in part because private-sector analysts were so bearish about growth. If those analysts had been correct, the Fed might have tightened sooner and dampened the economy's growth momentum.

One final lesson from the forecasting errors of the past six or seven years is that they underscore the need for reporters to take into account the track record of economists they interview. The press should not be a megaphone for erroneous predictions of doom or undue optimism. The press needs to pay attention to who is right and who is not.

Get the Latest News and Research on Liberal Media Bias

MRC NEWSLETTERS

★ The MRC's popular e-mail report, **CyberAlert**, notifies readers of the latest instances of liberal media bias — often just hours after it occurs.

★ Bi-weekly issues of **Notable Quotables** keep readers abreast of the most outrageous, sometimes humorous quotes from the liberal media. **NQ** is very popular with media insiders.

★ **Media Reality Check** is a weekly – sometimes daily – fax report that covers major news stories distorted or ignored by the national media.

★ The MRC's membership newsletter, **FLASH**, is a monthly eight-pager packed with photographs and interesting bits of the most ludicrous examples of media bias that occurred over the month, along with columns by L. Brent Bozell III, Special Reports, and details on recent MRC findings.

BEST-SELLING BOOKS

★ The explosive book **Pattern of Deception: The Media's Role in the Clinton Presidency** assembles a mountain of evidence proving how the liberal media, especially the television networks, promoted the Clinton agenda, both during his campaign and his presidency.

★ **How To Identify, Expose and Correct Liberal Media Bias** includes a detailed explanation of how to identify eight types of media bias complete with real life examples of each, plus step-by-step instructions on how to analyze news stories and conduct studies proving the liberal bias.

Order form on the following page.

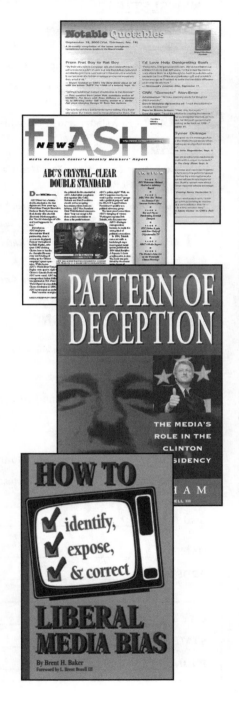

Be One of the First to Know!

NEWSLETTERS

☐ *Notable Quotables* – Bi-weekly newsletter / year's subscription
   ___MEMBERS $30*   ___NON-MEMBERS $40

☐ *CyberAlert* – **FREE** – Your e-mail address: _____

☐ *Media Reality Checks* - Weekly (sometimes daily) fax report
   FREE – Your facsimile number:(_____) _____

☐ *FLASH* – Newsletter and *Yearly Membership – ___$25

BOOKS

☐ *Pattern of Deception: The Media's Role in the Clinton Presidency*
   ___MEMBERS $12.95   ___NON-MEMBERS $18.95

☐ *How to Identify, Expose & Correct Liberal Media Bias*
   ___MEMBERS $12.95   ___NON-MEMBERS $18.95

☐ *And That's The Way It Isn't: A Reference Guide to Media Bias*
   ___MEMBERS $9.95   ___NON-MEMBERS $14.95

☐ *Out of Focus: Network TV & the American Economy*
   ___MEMBERS $9.95   ___NON-MEMBERS $14.95

*MEMBERSHIP OPTIONS

___$25   ___$50   ___$75 $ _____

MRC is a 501(c)3 nonprofit research and education foundation. All donations to the MRC are tax-deductible. A receipt will be mailed to you for tax purposes.

BOOKS   Add costs checked above $ _____

NEWSLETTERS   Add costs checked above $ _____

                                    TOTAL - plus $3 S&H $ _____

PAYMENT OPTIONS

☐ **CHECK:** Please make it payable to the *Media Research Center*

☐ **CREDIT CARD**   ___ Visa   ___Mastercard   ___AmEx   ___Discover

Name as appears on card _____

Card Number _____ Exp. Date _____

NAME _____

ADDRESS _____

_____

CITY _____

STATE_____ ZIP _____

PHONE_____

Mail this form & payment to:
Circulation Manager
Media Research Center
325 S. Patrick Street
Alexandria, VA 22314

or call (800) 672-1423

You can also order online at
www.MediaResearch.org